STUDENT VOICES
THE WRITER'S RANGE

Hans P. Guth
San Jose State University

Wadsworth Publishing Company
A Division of Wadsworth, Inc.

For Ingrid, Michael, Susan, and Paul Guth,
                my favorite student writers

English Editor: Angela M. Gantner

Editorial Assistant: Julie Johnson

Production Editor: Michael G. Oates

Print Buyer: Barbara Britton

Managing Designer: James Chadwick

Interior Design: Rogondino & Associates

Compositor: Rogondino & Associates

Cover Design: James Chadwick

Cover Illustration: © 1989 Michael Surles

© 1989 by Wadsworth, Inc. All rights reserved. No part of this book may be reproduced, stored in a retrieval system, or transcribed, in any form or by any means, electronic, mechanical, photocopying, recording, or otherwise, without the prior written permission of the publisher, Wadsworth Publishing Company, Belmont, California 94002, a division of Wadsworth, Inc.

Printed in the United States of America   49

2 3 4 5 6 7 8 9 10 - - - - - 93 92 91 90

Library of Congres Cataloging-in-Publication Data

Guth, Hans Paul
       Student Voices.

  1. College readers. 2. College prose, American.
3. English language--Rhetoric. I. Title.
PE1417.G877 1989   808'.0427   89-5266
ISBN 0-534-11724-4

Table of Contents

Part One: Writers At Work

Triggering: Why We Write 4
Gathering: Mobilizing Your Resources 10
Gathering: The Programed Search 22
Shaping: From Notes To Draft 25
Revising: Writing And Rewriting 31

Part Two: The Writer's Tasks

1 **Experience: Telling Your Story** 39
   Home, Sweet Home 40
   Free at Last 42
   Glamour 44
   Burn 47
   My Parents, Myself 48
   Writing Topics 1 51

2 **Observation: The Closer Look** 53
   The Song and the Dance 54
   Fourth of July 56
   The Fire Seeder 57
   What Is Wrong? 61
   Writing Topics 2 63

3 **Exposition: Let Me Explain** 65
   Tree Cutting, Country Style (process) 66
   Life in the Country (comparison / contrast) 68
   Wolves Mate for Life—Do You? (comparison /contrast) 71
   And in This Corner! (classification) 74
   "Bang! Zap! and Pow!": Punk in Retrospect (classification) 77
   Writing Topics 3 80

4 **The Active Reader: Writing from Sources** 81
   Man with a Mission 82
   The Computer as Teacher 86
   The Artificial Heart 89
   Writing Topics 4 94

5 **Definition: Weighty Words** 95
   Macho 96
   Doublespeak 98
   Secular Humanism 100
   Fundamentalism 102
   Writing Topics 5 105

6 **Argument: Pro and Con** 107
   Motorcycle Helmets 108
   The *Goldene Medinah* 111
   Drugs on the Job 113
   Whose Right to Life? 116
   Home Care or Institutional Care? 119
   Writing Topics 6 122

7 **Persuasion: The Power of Words** 124
   For the Sake of Appearances 125
   The Strong and the Rugged 127

Marriage: Bond or Bondage? 130
Justice 133
Go in Peace 135
Writing Topics 7 137

Part Three: Writing Across the Curriculum

8 Science Writing: The Uses and Abuses of Science 141
Was Granddad a Monkey? 142
Ice-Minus: The Chilling Effect 144
Fighting the "I Feel Fat" Diseases in the Schools 149
Whose Children Are These? 152
Writing Topics 8 155

9 Media Watch: The Critical Viewer 157
Soap Opera: The Modern Tragedy 158
Cashing In: A Television Perspective of Business 160
Realism and Ratings 162
The Last Temptation 164
Writing Topics 9 168

10 Social Issues: The Unfinished Agenda 170
Pink Collar Workers 171
Between Two Worlds 173

A Complex Issue 176
Rape 178
Pictures from My Mother's Trip to Hell 180
Writing Topics 10 183

11 Literature: The Responsive Reader 185
Today We Have Naming of Parts 186
Kate Chopin: Precursor of Modern Literature 188
Hemingway and the World of Illusion 189
Ramona—Fact or Fiction? 192
Writing Topics 11 197

Part Four: Essays for Peer Review

12 Evaluation: Editor for a Day 200
The Cruelty of Children's Athletics 201
Today's Homeless 202
The Essence of Practicality 204
An Introduction to Prejudice 206
Sometimes a Hidden Cancer 208

Introduction

The purpose of this collection is to provide models and inspiration for student writers. The student papers included here were worth writing and are worth reading. Among them, you should find at least some and perhaps many that have something to say to you as the reader. They may dramatize an issue for you, make you reconsider familiar assumptions, or broaden your understanding of people and ideas. These papers will have served their purpose if they make you think, if they make you want to write, and if they teach you something about good writing.

This collection reflects some basic beliefs about how and what students learn in successful writing courses. To profit from the opportunity to write and to learn by writing, consider guidelines like the following:

- *Learn to tap the untapped potential.* We are all born with a gift for language; we have resources of understanding, imagination, and wit that we need to learn to use and trust. The student writers in this collection have found a voice. They have found the confidence to say what is on their minds, to make themselves heard.

- *Trust the power of the good example.* Books like the *Harbrace Handbook* once used student papers mainly as horrible examples, creating a negative mindset that many teachers and students were unable to overcome. The student papers here are not meant to be perfect models, but many of the writers are very good at what they do. They show what students can do when they have found a reason to write, when they care enough to work up the material for a paper, and when they learn to pull the material into shape.

- *Think of professional writers (and your teachers) as fellow writers.* One purpose of this collection is to help bridge the gap between student writing and the prose of pros. Shakespeare got his start by rewriting other people's plays. Faulkner was once a student in a college writing class (getting Cs). The writing in this volume comes from classes ranging from basic writing through freshman composition to junior level courses and seminars where future teachers take on some of the writing tasks they will soon assign to their own students.

- *Develop your sense of audience.* Writing is not meant to be dropped down the well. When you see how you and others react to the student papers in this collection, you will be better able to project how readers will react to your own writing. Increasingly, students in writing classes write for their peers as well as for their instructors; they increasingly reach a larger audience through informal class publications and the like.

More than other teachers, writing teachers come to know their students as people, with personalities, agendas, and loyalties of their own. Like other writing teachers, I vividly remember many of the students who over the years have kept alive my faith in the power of the written word. I am thankful for their youthful enthusiasm, their candor, their perseverance, and their good humor. (One student labeled the last assignment in the course "Assignment #1,567,963.") Of the many students who have given me permission to use or adapt their writing, I want to thank especially Catherine Russell, Kelly Shannon Pritchett, Michael Carter, Cathy Powers, Torin Hussey, Michael Olson, Takuya Ugji, Jack Quinton, John Newman, Virginia Longshore, Julie A. Carter, Mary Ellison, Colleen Mari Scanlan, Sharette Giese, Mark Van Epps, Angelica Vasquez, Sandra Bouslaugh, Nancy Tepperman, Maureen Barney, Todd Marvin, Laurel Gardner, Sherry Van Zante, Marti Zeman, and David Carlisle.

Hans Guth

Part One

Writers At Work

How do writers produce work that is worth writing and worth reading? Manuals and guides for writers are full of advice, but one step is basic: We have to overcome the "reluctant-writer" syndrome. Reluctant writers put the job off till the very last minute, and even then their heart isn't in it. They write the first and only draft late at night before a paper or a project is due. In the words of one disillusioned writing teacher, the one incentive that keeps them going is the knowledge that the "damn thing is due at 9:30 Monday morning."

What with the pressure of college work, outside work, and campus social life or family obligations, the reluctant-writer syndrome is a very easy pattern to slide into. It is also totally different from how real writers work.

Real writers become involved in a subject. They begin to think about it and worry about it—they are thinking about it when they pretend to be listening politely to what you are saying about dorm food or the Big Game. They start working up the subject—they "read up" on it; they start collecting clippings and quotable quotes. They start talking about it, getting into arguments with a roommate or spouse. They develop some firm hunches or tentative conclusions, but they also change their minds on some key points as they stumble onto unsuspected evidence. They turn to people who should know for the inside story.

Very few real writers write a piece off the tops of their heads, in a fury of creation. They may in fact get bogged down and develop a case of the writer's blues. But eventually they start pulling their material together; things start to fall into place. While working out a first or intermediate draft, many of them experience a "writer's high"—a feeling of excitement or elation as the paper or article begins to take shape. Many writers will circulate a rough first copy for feedback from friends, editors, or reviewers. At this point, writers have to steel themselves for criticism—some of it flattering, some of it painful, some of it truly dense or infuriating, and all of it well worth thinking about. Now is the time for second thoughts, for some serious rethinking and revision.

Writing that has gone through this kind of process is real writing. To make sure your own writing is true writing and not pap, try out some of the techniques and procedures used by real writers.

TRIGGERING: WHY WE WRITE

No one wants to eat in a restaurant where the chef hates to cook. Good writing reflects some personal interest, some personal commitment, on the part of the writer. Something set the process of writing in motion; something brought it on. Even if the writing was an assigned task, the writer found the "personal connection"—something that made the task worthwhile.

Some of the best writing we read comes from the heart (as well as from the head). You will do some of your own best writing when you feel you need to tell your side of the story, when you feel you need to respond to some misrepresentation, when you want to defend a decision or a policy that has been unfairly criticized. Early in a writing project, clarify your purpose—give some serious thought to what you are trying to do.

Planning Reports   One of the best titles an author ever used for a guide for writers was *Writing with a Purpose.* Make it a practice to spell out your own purpose for a paper in a preliminary planning report. What are you trying to do? What do you expect the paper to do for you as the writer and for your reader? Where is your material going to come from? Do you have a tentative strategy or overall plan?

What kind of paper is each of the following planning reports sketching out? Do you think either paper would mean something to you as a reader?

City Slickers/Country Bumpkins

I'm going to write a comparison/contrast paper on urban and rural life. I plan to focus on the quality of life these two environments provide for the rearing of children. I personally know of several couples who have left California, sacrificing earning power and job opportunities for a better place to raise their children. I plan to explore this idea: Are our country's rural areas a better place to raise children? There are others who move from the city to rural areas looking for a cohesive community. Are rural dwellers more involved in each other's lives? And there are those, motivated by fear, who leave the city in search of a crime-free environment where their odds of becoming a victim of crime is decreased. Is the crime rate in rural areas lower? I hope to take a serious look at these issues and cause my readers to think.

Just Say No

There is a lot of media pressure and right-wing preaching about drugs. It is an oversimplification to a complex problem: "Just say no." It seems so cut-and-dry. A lot of things are ignored. Different drugs bring different addictions. The worst addiction can be that of the recreational user. A lot of times the damage is not life-shattering or even noticeable on the surface. But sooner or later you have to pay for the dance.

I was mentally, though not physically addicted to methamphetamine. I did not lose a job or my family. However, in little ways, it ate at me. It chipped away at my self-esteem, made me justify things I would never have considered sober. To best let readers see how important this was for me, I am going to take them on a little ride to hell in suburbia.

The Personal Connection How can you discover some of the motives that make writers write? One way is to write about something that truly matters to you in your own experience. Many writing teachers tell us that everyone has a story to tell. We have all grown up in a setting or with people who helped shape what we are; we have had to cope with things that were difficult to deal with; we have experienced something that became a turning point in our lives. We often write to share an experience; to make our readers understand.

The following student paper stays close to personal experience. Can you see that the paper had a special personal meaning for the author? Read the paper in order to answer questions like the following:

- What kind of person is speaking to you in this paper?

- What was the writer's purpose? What did writing this paper do for the writer?

- What did reading this paper do for you as the reader? Do you provide a good audience for this writer? Why or why not?

Angry Independence

I find it frightening at times when I stop to think about the anger I feel toward both sides of my family. Although a majority of the time it remains submerged, my feeling often rears its head, creating many actions and mistakes caused by an angry assertion of myself. The emotional effects of frustration, trial and error, and resentment that I felt during my younger years, and those portrayed in Lillian Hellman's essay "An Only Child," I found astoundingly similar.

I too am an only child born into an unstable household. My father was frowned upon by my mother's side of the family who viewed him as unfit for her, not because of financial standing, but rather because he was the black sheep within his own family. The marriage was a trade--my mother wanting to expand her wings outside the state of Georgia, and my father wanting to reconcile himself with his family. The fact that he was in the Foreign Service and she was from one of the more predominant families within the community made a wedding the perfect solution, though neither will admit this to the other.

After two years of the newlyweds struggling to retain a marriage, I was conceived in an "attempt to calm your father's temperament and restlessness," as was quoted to me during a rare mother-to-daughter, heart-to-heart talk. I was born overseas and was to remain there, settling into the routine of moving every time I felt secure enough to call our house my home. So began the buildup of my resentment. The insecurities which I felt as a result of traveling, changing schools, houses, and friends approximately every two years led to one of the hardest struggles of my youth.

When I was twelve, it was decided that a move back to the United States would bring a welcome change. My father put in his request, and was given the first available post, Washington, D.C. We settled just outside the city in northern Virginia, and it was shortly thereafter that my parents agreed to a divorce. At the time, it was not really traumatic for me. Divorce was "in" in America and so many of my classmates were experiencing the same thing. I even felt a sense of happiness about it because, one, there would be no more fighting; and two, it gave me something in common with many of my peers. However, at the same time I also felt the guilt of it possibly being my fault and the resentment of being moved once again.

I saw my father only twice during the year between the divorce and my mother's remarriage. During that time I had withdrawn myself and become independent from both of them: My mother had her own new life, and my father seemed to feel that his signature on a check was a sufficient role for him to play. I then became very involved with school activities such as government, cheerleading, band, and the maintenance of my grades to be able to participate in them. I felt at my happiest during that time of my life. I had at last been given the time to earn the popularity and respect I had wanted for so long among my peers. Everything was running smoothly and things were going my way until it was announced that my stepfather had been offered a promotion. The catch was that we would be moving once again, this time to California.

I was outraged and fully prepared to rebel. How could my mother be so prepared to make me give up everything I had accomplished to follow a man I didn't even like? I confronted her with the fact that I had moved all of my life and that I was not prepared to leave what I felt was my home. Her reaction was one of shock. It was then that I realized that in the midst of the whirl in her life, she had stopped the clock on my aging process, for after the shock had worn off, I was informed that I had no choice because I was under age and in her legal custody.

My mother and stepfather lived in California for a full year before I finally joined them, and I have since discovered that they dislike California. Our plans are to make another move in the fall.

Targeting the Audience   Much of the writing we encounter we can place on a spectrum from the personal to the public. At one end of the spectrum, we find writing whose main focus is on personal memories, thoughts, and feelings. The writers may be writing mainly for their own satisfaction—to "get something out of their systems," to come to terms with something important to them. Often they are not aiming at a specific target audience. They hope for a sympathetic hearing from readers who need not have had exactly similar experiences but who care about what has happened to other people.

At the other end of the spectrum is the kind of writing that targets a specific audience and aims at results. The writers may tell us what they have personally learned about the subject, but they tell us in order to make us change our minds. Much writing aims at a definite practical goal—a vote, a sale, a subscription, a job, a promotion. Knowing the audience and reaching the audience then become high priorities for the writer.

The following paragraph sets up a writing situation involving three very different audiences. In responding to a controversial drug raid at a local high school, you might choose to write to (1) the school authorities, (2) the parents of the students, or (3) the parents themselves. Study the account of the incident and then the student letters triggered by it:

> The school authorities in a local high school have collaborated with the police to place undercover narcotics agents in classes to mingle and make friends with the students. After six weeks of investigation, fifteen students have been arrested on charges of selling cocaine or marijuana. They have been taken in handcuffs to Juvenile Hall, where most of them still remain several weeks later. School officials defend their action by explaining that it was necessary to crack down and provide a deterrent to other students. Many of the parents involved are furious, complaining that their children face expulsion and permanent damage to their future careers.

The students writing the following letters are role-playing a concerned parent, the principal of the school, or a concerned fellow student. As you read the letters, ask yourself: How did the writers size up the chosen audience? What assumptions do they make about the way the audience is likely to respond? How effectively do you think they reach the intended audience?

1. Dear Principal: I feel strongly about your high school policy of using undercover police masquerading as students in order to apprehend those using and selling drugs. Education can exist only in an environment of trust among students, teachers, and administrators. Students must believe that the adults in the school are open and honest with them and that their friends are not lurking behind corners and in dark hallways in order to inform on them. Your cooperation with the undercover drug operation violates the responsibility of the school to promote the good faith essential for mutual trust.

   A student should feel secure in a school environment in order to develop the ability to see many points of view and to resist simple solutions. The courage to challenge the status quo and the powers that be needs a safe setting to develop. If students have to watch what they say and be careful where their questions might lead them, learning cannot take place.

   Many movies popular with young people mirror their belief that adults lie and betray, and that they are ultimately the enemy. Policies like those you instituted to stem the tide of drug use reinforce this unwillingness to enter the world of the untrustworthy grown-up.

2. Dear Parent: As the principal of Jefferson High, I sympathize with all of your concerns for your children because of the recent arrests. Let me attempt to explain what led the administration to believe that this crackdown was necessary. We are at a critical point in our history at Jefferson High. While unexcused student absences and general misconduct are at an all-time high, the staff is smaller now than when we had three hundred fewer students. We have had to trim the counseling staff and have half as many custodians as before. We don't have the funds to provide the student services and educational programs that once made our school one of the best in the area.

Yet, day in day out we do our best. Our talented staff tries to be everywhere at once. Our SAT scores are high. Our music department was ranked one of the best in the state, as was our science department.

Unfortunately, in our proud garden of accomplishments, there exists a thorn that threatens to destroy everything we have done for our students. That thorn is drug abuse. Drugs and education don't mix. Despite our best efforts, drugs have become more prevalent at Jefferson High. I'm sure that you are aware of the many drug-related problems we have experienced in the last few years. I've called a father at work and told him that his daughter was in the hospital with a drug overdose. We have had a drug-related car accident that took the life of one student and left another permanently disabled.

These were the considerations on my mind when I decided to let the police infiltrate the drug scene at Jefferson High. My first responsibility to you and the students is to provide a safe, positive, drug-free learning environment. We are sending out strong and clear messages on our stance against drugs. Won't you join us in the battle?

3. Dear Students: Regardless of where you stand on the issue of the recent undercover investigation, the fact remains that drug use is illegal, punishable by law. Drug use can lead to addiction, physical decline, even death. The law is supposed to disregard what socio-economic group you came from and will not protect you from jail or a police record because you are a star athlete or a straight-A student.

   You are now at an age where you are making more and more decisions on you own. You may decide to use drugs because you feel you are old enough to handle them, or because friends use them without obvious negative results. But remember that you need to know the facts. Educate yourself. Read about drug use; talk to a counselor or health teacher. Don't take the advice of your peers or what you see in the media as gospel truth. Only by truly educating yourself can you make an adult choice. If you as individuals choose to take drugs, sell drugs, or otherwise act unlawfully, you must expect to reap the consequences of your actions eventually. It is one of the repercussions of becoming an adult.

Your Turn: Is there something that *you* want to tell one of these three hypothetical audiences? Go on record with your thoughts or reactions. Address one of the three groups involved.

GATHERING: MOBILIZING YOUR RESOURCES

A crucial step in any writing project, large or small, is the search for promising material. Staffers for a newsmagazine do not write about the homeless on the spur of the moment; they research an article to gather data, to read up on the subject, to talk to people in the know. The quality and extent of the input at this prewriting stage helps determine whether the finished product will be superficial and opinionated or substantial and well-grounded.

When we work up the material for a substantial piece of writing, we try to mobilize what we already know, and we set out in search of what we need to learn. Writers have their own ways of working up material, ranging from the very informal or happenstance to the very well-organized or structured. Study and practice some of the material-gathering techniques used by successful writers.

Journal Writing Many professional writers keep a log, diary, or journal. They have some way to record and store observations, thoughts passing through their minds, memories. A writer's log is for actual writing what an incubator is for chickens—an entry often becomes the germ of an idea for a full-grown piece of writing. At the same time, keeping a log or journal gets you into the habit of getting things down on paper—of putting your thoughts and feelings into words.

Look at the following examples of journal entries. Which of them already contain the germ of an idea for a paper? How might the entry be developed into a full-grown paper? Which of these entries bring to mind memories or observations that you could use in journal entries of your own?

Whales

The giant blue whale that washed up on shore is one of those things I wish I'd seen in person. I'm certain that the magnitude of its size is lost upon anyone who can't actually stand next to it and feel how small and unimportant we can be in comparison. It's typical of human nature, though, that some people who went to look at it carved their initials in the putrifying flesh and cut off "souvenirs." That type of behavior is representative of humankind's disrespect for other creatures and the environment in general. Yes, I know the animal was dead. But it seems to me that something that huge, that beautiful, that rare, deserves something more than our regular lack of sanctity.

Dreams

I dreamed last night I was in a bright red air balloon with my father, who had in reality been dead for many years. We skimmed along for a time, so high all we could see were blurred shapes and patches of color, when suddenly the balloon began to collapse and we started to fall. I hadn't realized that other people were in the balloon with us until I heard screaming all around me. "My God, we're done for!" someone cried out. Trees and houses and vast bodies of water sped below us, coming closer and closer, and in my mind I saw the balloon impaled on the edge of a black roof of a house below. Then we moved beyond the house toward another body of water. My father shouted to me, "When we land, roll so the impact won't hurt you." The water shattered like glass, shards piercing my shoulders and face. But I did just as my father had instructed, rolling across the surface of the water like a beach ball and discovered to my relief and delight that I was all right. He had saved me.

Motherhood

I get up every day in the middle of the night to feed my son, too tired to have a "meaningful" experience with him. In the morning, I am still tired and I discover that instead of doing the ordinary things I used to take for granted, I now must wait until he is asleep or preoccupied before I can accomplish them. I revel in the moments we have together where I feel there is some "connection," where we are communicating on the smallest of levels. Yet even when I am tired, wishing I could luxuriate in the warm bed with the paper and coffee for an hour or so instead of getting up to change a diaper, I feel this tremendous wash of tenderness for the chubby-fisted, pink-cheeked person in the crib.

School

When I think of school, I begin to feel tired. It's not a sleepy tired but more of a tired that comes about when something doesn't work, but it didn't really matter because that wasn't your direction. I'm a quiet, shy, and reserved person. School calls for discussion, input, and voicing of opinions that often turn into heated discussions that lead nowhere. These activities are necessary so the teacher has a better idea of what he/she needs to do. I think it's the way a class should work, but it's not the way I am. It burns me out hearing people argue and get nothing out of it but a dry, sticky throat, a pair of chapped lips, and a headache that will last them until their next dispute. People aren't taught to listen. Instead they are urged to talk and foolishly blurt their opinions on topics they know nothing about.

Relatives

My grandmother tells stories about the life of a little girl growing up in a small town in Minnesota

among people of German origin early in the century. As
Grandmother says, it is important for the younger generations to know what life in the past was like in
order to take advantage of and appreciate life in the
present. It also prepares us (the younger generation)
for possible reoccurrences of events such as the Great
Depression. I am told over and over that I do not know
how good I have things, or "someday you're going to
want that plastic bag," in reference to my wastefulness
compared to her own resourceful recycling abilities
stemming from her lack of money while growing up and
during the Depression. I appreciate Grandma's sometimes
harsh words and warnings. Someday I will be thanking
her for that second meal, an extra portion of food
made, when her voice returns to admonish, "Someday
you're going to wish you had that."

From journal entries like these, it is only one step to the kind of paper we call a *vignette*—a brief account of an incident or a person. Though told briefly, a vignette usually already has a point or makes us think. Does the following brief student paper make you think? As you finish the paper, what thoughts are going through your mind?

The Year of the Turkey

Autumns in southern California are mild, so it
wasn't odd that while the Thanksgiving turkey roasted,
most of the family was out back eating antipasta beneath the avocado and fruit trees. Granma always
cooked too much--everybody said so--and every holiday
the tables groaned with turkey, ham, and ricotta ravi-
oli, sweet bell peppers and dried tomatoes soaked in
wine and garlic, apple and pecan pies. One year--I
must have been twelve--while the rest of the family was
out back drinking Granpa's wine, I was in front reading. I didn't immediately notice the woman coming up
the walk until she was right in front of me. She explained that she was from the downtown mission and was
collecting donations to feed the hungry--did we have any
extra food? It seemed logical to me, so I suggested
that she take the turkey; after all, I explained, we
had plenty. She was skeptical but I insisted. (I remember thinking how awful it must be to be hungry.)
Shortly thereafter I heard all kinds of yelling and

Granpa came running out of the house yelling that we'd been robbed, that some bastard had stolen our turkey. I tried to explain but before I could finish, everyone was cursing and screaming about how stupid I was. My aunt shook me until my glasses fell off my face. I didn't have a chance to say anything else but I remember thinking that they didn't see me; all they could see was the empty turkey platter. Now, everybody laughs about the year I gave away the turkey, just as they laughed about the fact that I was always behind a book. My children will never hear that laugh. They never will because I don't think what people believe in, what they think is right, is funny.

Your Turn: Write an autobiographical vignette that has a special personal meaning for you. Pack it with detail that will make the setting, the people, or the event come to life for your reader.

Brainstorming Like a supercomputer with a tremendously capacious memory, the human mind stores a vast array of data, events, faces, details, concepts, and images. From the memory banks of the brain, an effective writer retrieves the material that relates to his or her current topic. Brainstorming is a technique for activating the retrieval process. When brainstorming, we let our memory range freely, jogging it with the right stimulus word or the right cue, following a chain of association where it might lead. We allow images, details, and ideas to rise to the surface, to "pop up" on our mental screens.

In successful brainstorming, one memory or one idea leads to another. Keep asking yourself: "What do I know? What do I remember? What comes to mind?" What comes to mind when you hear a term like *redneck*? Here is one student's brainstorming of the word:

```
Redneck:
George Wallace--arch-conservatism--Strom Thurmond, Jessie
Helms
Beer-drinking--stills--moonshine--Federal investigations
Swamps--vigilantism--shotguns--hounds--hangings
Alligators--armadilloes--turtles--moss--humidity
Racist--KKK--Jackson, MS
Good Ol'Boys--BBQ--Country Music--Square Dancing--Texas
2-step
Cowboy boots and hats--string-ties--polyester suits--
mother-of-pearl buttons--pick-up trucks
Macho--chauvinist--keep the "little woman" barefoot and
pregnant
```

```
Shanty houses--poor white trash--greasy pork and turnip
greens--chicken and dumplings--biscuits with gravy--
grits--cornpone--L'il Abner
Baptists--Segregation--Snake-oil Salesmen--TV evangelists
```

What kind of paper do you think will come out of this preliminary brainstorming? What questions would you like to ask the author? What advice might you give?

Your Turn: Brainstorm a term like *corruption, nostalgia, Romantic, racism, relationships.*

Clustering Clustering, like brainstorming, lets our minds follow up associations. But the ideas that come to mind branch out from a central core (or rather cluster around it), so that a tentative pattern or design already takes shape as we jot down our thoughts. The idea behind clustering is that ideas are not really stored in our minds in totally miscellaneous fashion. There are already tentative and possible connections, and writing allows us to explore and develop these.

Here is a very simple cluster from Gabriele Rico's *Writing the Natural Way*:

Here is the writing based on this cluster, by a very young person who had already had her share of trouble:

Flame

```
    Flame is how I feel right now--so bitter I can
taste it.   I can't tell you how upset and fed up with
life I am.   I feel like something is tearing up inside
me.   If I look back on the reasons, I guess it's all
my own fault.   People light their own fires.
```

Here is another somewhat more developed cluster from Rico's book:

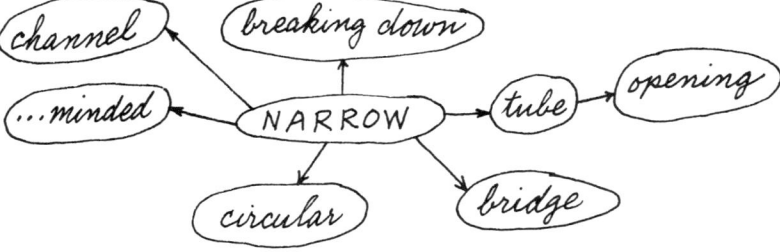

Here is the writing based on this cluster:

Narrow

Narrow is a word that has no particular meaning to me. It's not that I don't want to write, it's just that, when I think of narrow, I associate it with narrow bridges, narrow channels, generally just narrow openings. For example, a narrow-minded person does not seem like a well-rounded person. Narrowing down to something is a funneling down or reducing down. Narrowing the chances or narrowing down the competition is like breaking down the resistance, which is what this clustering exercise just did to me. I realize I was wrong about what I said in the first sentence. The word, narrow, does have meanings to me, after all.

Reading Notes A big difference between the amateur and the professional writer is that the pros constantly seem to be taking notes. They are constantly jotting down facts and figures, revealing details, or quotable quotes. In particular, they *read* more attentively than other people, noting things that will prove useful in their own writing. Once they focus on a topic, they "read up" on it, preparing detailed reading notes.

Study the following reading notes for a paper triggered by the recent spate of proposals for English-only or English-first legislation. More and more students whose first language was not English do not learn English well enough to succeed in school. Should they be taught history and math in their own language until they have a chance to catch up? Should their parents have the benefit of bilingual ballots or laws?

This writer's note-taking begins with some personal memories and firsthand observations. He then starts jotting down expert opinion and personal testimony from his reading. Some of the ideas he puts in his own words (paraphrase or indirect quotation). But many of the key quotations appear verbatim, in quotation marks, with a mix of short excerpts and medium-length quotations.

English First?

I remember as a child hearing different languages spoken in my neighborhood. The Japanese mother would call her children for dinner in Japanese; Cindy's father would call her in his thick German accent; Nancy's parents would talk in Black English, and my mother would occasionally bring us snacks and make remarks to me in French. But the kids all spoke to each other in English. Many children had parents who did not want them to learn the parents' native language, and therefore did not allow their children to learn it--for fear it would hinder them from learning English.

When I went to renew my driver's license, an older man was assisted on his written test by his son who translated the questions into their native language. I watched him (them) take the eye exam. And the son continued to translate for him the questions being asked by the DMV personnel! The woman administering the test passed this gentleman, but commented as they left that it was incredible to have to pass people who spoke no English.

European countries have road signs--for one way, pedestrian crossing, danger--that do not use language.

Historical background: James Stalker notes that "Benjamin Franklin expressed the fear that German would be so prevalent in Pennsylvania that the legislature would need interpreters" (19).

In Pennsylvania, there were German bilingual schools in the late nineteenth century, and newspapers printed in German were common in parts of the midwest and the east. According to Stalker "the Louisiana constitution allowed the publication of laws in French . . . until about seventy years ago" (20).

Challenges to bilingual education: President Reagan's Secretary of Education said in 1985 that the bilingual learning program, costing over a billion dollars in 17 years was "a failed path" (Time 55). Under Reagan 4% of the federal funds for bilingual education were utilized for other methods, such as ESL and English immersion. On April 28, 1988, this changed. Now 25% of federal money will go to alternative methods. The majority of the money for bilingual education comes from state capitals, though, and there the bilingual lobbies are strong. In an article by the Wall Street Journal, the bilingual lobby is described as composed of "statehouse enthusiasts, school-district program administrators, teacher-training staffs at feeder colleges, producers of classroom materials, and some Mexican-American spokesmen" (20).

```
          Legal background:   Passage of the Bilingual Educa-
     tion Act in 1968.  After this came a decision in 1974
     from the Supreme Court which interpreted the Civil
     Rights Act in terms of helping bilingual education
     (Smithson in Oakland Tribune Article, Feb. 13, 1988).
          Nicolas Sanchez (Hispanic educator) writes in The
     Education Digest why he is against most methods of bi-
     lingual education, though he opposes English as an offi-
     cial language:
               I consider to be bilingual a person who is
               fluent in two different languages.  Therefore, I
               would have to argue that many, if not most,
               Hispanics in this country are not bilingual.
               Usually they rapidly alternate between English
               and Spanish . . . Hispanics find it almost
               impossible to conduct a conversation exclusively
               in Spanish (42).
          Many young Hispanics speak a dialect that is neither
     Spanish nor English, but a combination of the two.  He
     feels "teaching English should be the main linguistic
     goal of our schools . . . that is what they can teach
     effectively . . ." (43).
```

As you study these notes, where does the writer seem to be headed? What questions arise in your mind that these materials leave unanswered? What would you try to find out from further reading?

Interviews   What opportunities and what obstacles lie ahead for young women pursuing a nontraditional career? One obvious place to look for answers is magazines like *Ms.* or *Working Woman,* where in a given issue you might find the story of a woman who became a district attorney or a report on what happened to women who worked in investment firms and found their jobs jeopardized after the crash of '87. Another promising source of material is the grass roots testimony of women in the workplace whom you might be able to interview.

Obviously, some people are too harried or too defensive to make good prospects for an interview. However, most student interviewers find that many people are pleased when someone genuinely cares about their experiences and opinions. Effective interviewers often put the interviewee at ease with questions showing a genuine interest in the person. They then work up to the more difficult or probing questions. They give those being interviewed a chance to talk and to think—allowing them to follow up a predictable or evasive answer with a revealing one.

Study the questions and answers in the following sample interview. What questions does it raise in *your* mind that you would like to follow up? What kind of paper do you think the interview might lead to?

Woman Engineer

Question: What is your background and what or who inspired you to become an engineer?

Answer: After high school graduation I began college as a pre-med student because at that time I wanted to become a doctor. During those summers I held jobs in electronics and mechanical assembly that had to do with lasers. The summer job turned out to be a two-year stay, and this is when I switched horses in mid-stream and went into an engineering major. The two major influences were my father and my boss; both of them were engineers. My boss had said, "You really like this stuff and you are good at it. Why don't you get a degree?"

Some background that was helpful for me when growing up was that we, my brothers and one sister, were always encouraged to do well academically. I never felt I couldn't be good in mathematics or in physics. We were guided, or forced as some of my brothers and sister would have said, to take a wide range or pretty heavy academic load through high school and college.

Question: How did you find it being in advanced science and mathematics courses in college? Did you find that you were the only female or just one of a few?

Answer: No, actually in the engineering classes about a third of all the classes that I was in had women in them. These women included majors in general engineering, mechanical engineering, industrial engineering, and civil engineering.

Question: Have you had to overcome any specific obstacles in reaching your goal to become an engineer? Has anyone ever turned you down for a job because someone figured that you cannot do the job?

Answer: No, actually I think that most women engineers in my field find the opposite. Some people might call it reverse discrimination because there are not very many women engineers around, so for a lot of companies, it is a feather in their cap to get a woman engineer on their staff.

Question: Why is that?

Answer: For one thing there is equal opportunity. So there must be some benefit to have a number of minorities and women on their staff, and women engineers are considered a minority. As for obstacles, there have been a number of them that I have seen. I don't know that they have been obstacles because I think I have found ways to get around them. One of the obstacles is the older male engineers who make you feel that you have to work twice as hard as your male counterpart to prove you know what you are doing. With the younger engineers, closer to my age, I find there is more acceptance because they have gone to school with other women students, which enables them not to have the same bias.

Question: Were you readily accepted as a woman engineer in you company?

Answer: I feel I am working in a very small and close-knit group, so I don't find it to be a problem at all. The problem I would like to point out is that sometimes you have very curious relationships with the other women you work with. You find some really strange reactions to your position. For the most part, I think the technical women have no problem because they understand where you are at. For example, I can remember one incident of going out to lunch with a group of women and we were all laughing and talking and making little comments. Later on, people were kidding around, and the next day someone came up to me and apologized. She said, "Oh, I am really sorry. I didn't know you were an engineer." I was really shocked because I didn't know how to react to that. I don't consider anyone just a secretary or just a . . . I find that people think that they are supposed to treat me differently because I hold a non-traditional position for a woman. I wonder if some women might feel resentment toward other women in these positions.

Question: What is your official title?

Answer: I am a product engineer. My responsibilities: I oversee an established product line all the way from its sub-assemblies to the final test and out the door. I deal with problems on producibility and cost effectiveness. I also have more engineering responsibilities.

Question: Do you have any advice you would like to give to any up-and-coming women engineers?

Answer: Yes. Don't be put off by any of the old stigmas and the old realities. There will be obstacles, but I also feel that they are there for everyone going into any field. For women in a male-dominated field I think there are some definite obstacles. You cannot pretend to say that we have all been liberated and everything is equal and everybody accepts you for what you can do. I say go in with your eyes open and accept some of the realities. I don't believe it helps to be really militant about it and point out to everyone that you are a woman. I am sure that they can see that when you walk through the door. In a lot of ways I think that it can hurt you more than you realize. The idea is to go in and show what you can do, even though some people say, "Well, sometimes people do not recognize that." If this happens I feel you are in the wrong place and should move on to someplace where it is recognized. That advice I would give to anybody, anywhere.

Much successful writing draws on the right mix of personal memory, alert first-hand observation, and purposeful reading. Often an effective paper will go from personal experience to similar experiences of others as discovered through reading or interviews. Often an effective paper will bring an issue to life by starting with expert opinion and then letting the reader hear the voices of people directly concerned. A resourceful writer seldom suffers from the beginner's problem of not having enough material, of not having enough to say. The experienced practitioner is more likely to suffer from an oversupply, requiring determined sifting and editing in order to produce a manageable paper.

GATHERING: THE PROGRAMED SEARCH

Some writers go about the gathering of material in an exceptionally determined fashion. They conduct a structured search, following a plan that often already foreshadows the structure of the paper. They may systematically look for the answers to questions that serve as a discovery frame—as a framework for systematic investigation.

For instance, in preparing a paper about a memorable event, or about a high point or a turning point in the writer's life, the writer might set out to ask the five storyteller's questions that follow:

- Setting—Where are we? What will it take to make your readers visualize the setting, the scene?

- People—Who are the key players in the drama? What do they look like; how do they talk and act?

- Situation—What led up to the event? What background or context do you need to fill in for your readers?

- Event—What happened? How did things come to a head? How can you dramatize the high point of the story?

- Point—What did you learn from the event? How did it change your thinking or your attitude? Why is it worth remembering?

Can you show how the following student paper conforms to the program sketched out in these five questions?

The Devil Made Me Do It

The house was one of those tract homes that are indistinguishable from their neighbors. It was always shadowy and smelled like a pantry. The room I had rented was down the hall, to the right. Coming home from football practice, I would timidly walk into the kitchen, make a bologna sandwich, and walk down the hall to eat it in my room, ready to put on a fake smile when I encountered the Westons, the couple who owned the house.

My parents and I had agreed that I should live, at least to start with, with a Christian family (it was more their idea than mine), my parents being fairly religious people. The Westons both looked alike: He wore sweaters all the time, wore glasses, and spoke and moved softly; she always wore drab skirts, was always smiling, and had a hairdo that looked twenty years out of style. They were always holding hands and prayed over the tiniest things. They often said things like "Praise the Lord" and welcomed me as a "fine young Christian man" the first day.

When I moved in, I had no idea of what to bring besides clothes and necessities (the only thing the Westons had specified was no loud music, so my stereo and extensive collection of rock and roll records were out). I decided to bring my comic book collection and all my fantasy and horror novels. I was then at the peak of my collecting and had six or seven shoe boxes with titles like Spiderman, Daredevil, Iron Man, and Moon Knight. After I finished lugging the boxes with comics and paperbacks into my new room, I asked the Westons if they wanted to check out their backroom, which was now mine. They said "No, that's your room" and smiled.

A week after I moved in, as I was walking down the hall munching my bologna sandwich on the way to my room, the Westons confronted me at the door to the room and said: "We'd like you to get rid of these . . . things." They pointed accusingly at the bookcase where my beloved books were stored. I looked at them in disbelief and said: "I'll do it in the morning." They said "No--right now." Without saying anything, I carefully carried each box across the street to my car, while the Westons stood by, looking distressed. When I approached the room after the last box was secure in my car, I saw the Westons kneeling, holding hands, and muttering prayers over the spot where my books had been. I remember slinking down the hall and into the bathroom, where I stayed until I heard them leave my room.

This event marked the beginning of my disillusionment with the kind of narrow religious attitude these people represented. I had been taught to think of them as the best kind of people: kind, decent. They sat glued to religious television, yet they couldn't stand to see a Daredevil cover sticking out above the top of a shoebox. The Devil was in their house, and they were going to cleanse the spot where he had dwelled.

Often the nature of the writing task helps the writer program the search for material. Suppose you are working on a paper comparing American and Japanese management styles. You might decide to look systematically for material for a point-by-point comparison focusing on such points as loyalty to the company, attitude toward workers, study of the competition, and long-range vs. short-range goals.

The following are a writer's preliminary notes for a pro-and-con paper. The writer has systematically lined up first the arguments for and then the arguments against making the wearing of protective helmets compulsory for riders of motorcycles. Can you see that this preliminary lining up of the pros and cons already provides a strong basic structure for the proposed paper? (See the finished paper later in this collection to discover how the writer used and modified this preliminary plan.)

Motorcycle Helmets

The Issue: Should protective helmets be required by law for all riders and passengers of motorcycles, motor scooters, mopeds and any other two or three-wheeled vehicles operated on public roads and highways?

Pros

1. Most motorcycle deaths and serious injuries are caused by injuries to the head. It is estimated that 20,000 lives could be saved nationally if all motorcycle drivers and passengers wore proper head protection.

2. 86% of the cost of treating motorcycle injuries is ultimately borne by the State as motorcyclists typically don't have the insurance or resources to pay their own care-- especially for head injuries where lengthy

Cons

1. Motorcycle riding in the open air is one of our last personal freedoms. If a person chooses to put themselves in harm's way there should be no law preventing it.

2. Helmets make it difficult to hear sirens and other road noises and would actually make riding less safe except in a very serious accident.

3. Many motorcyclists are free spirits who find helmets needlessly restrictive. They enjoy

hospitalization and surgery are required.

3. Insurance rates could be reduced for both motorcyclists and auto drivers if costly medical care and legal assistance could be reduced.

4. California auto drivers are required by law to wear seatbelts--why not protective devices for motorcyclists?

5. Auto drivers need to be spared the personal, lifelong, responsibility for having seriously hurt or killed another in a collision when it could have been prevented by adequate protection.

the elements--the wind in their hair--too much to accept such a restrictive device as a helmet.

4. Helmets are not comfortable. They are hot, sweaty contraptions that are tight, ill-fitting and plain uncomfortable.

5. Helmets are expensive. A good quality helmet costs $60 or more. Many motorcyclists are young people and students who can't afford such an expense.

6. Storing a helmet when not riding is a problem. Few motorcycles have a lockable storage area sufficient to hold a helmet.

Conclusion: All the reasons against requiring motorcycle helmets combined aren't worth the risk of a single life or the hurt and emotional pain of one auto driver who must live forever with the death or injury of another on his mind. The State has a vested interest in motorcycle safety since so many state dollars go for medical costs associated with accident injuries which are largely preventable. Driving a motorcycle, like an automobile, is a privilege, not a right. For that reason it is reasonable and appropriate to require helmets on all public roads.

SHAPING: FROM NOTES TO DRAFT

Good writers know how to organize their thinking. They know how to lay out their material in a way that makes sense to the reader. In a fruitful search, we do not proceed totally in the dark. We early develop a sense of direction. We have some key questions that guide our investigation, or we have some tentative ideas to check out. We do a rough sorting of our materials; we arrange them in some tentative order. As we go along, that tentative order firms up to become a definite strategy for organizing our writing.

The Master Plan When we organize our material, our goal is a master plan, a "grand design," that fits the material we have collected and that will make sense to the reader. What does such a master plan look like for a successful paper? Look at the prewriting notes and the first draft for the following paper attacking the stereotype of the dumb blonde. There is already a rough sorting out of material in the preliminary notes—going from notes of a media watcher to personal experience and then to relevant reading. Look for the master plan of the first draft:

- the media image (showing how widespread the stereotype really is)
- personal experience (explaining the writer's "personal connection" with the topic)
- evidence that *women* as well as men perpetuate the stereotype
- some basic physiological facts designed to counteract the stereotype

How is this final order different from the original order of material in the student's notes?

Prewriting: Notes

```
      The media stereotype:  blonde dream girl in tight
sweaters working as a maid for two leering men.  Blonde
airhead in Three's Company.  More current show:  Diane
in Cheers is smart and has a college education.  At
first she held her own, but in many later plots she was
shown to be arrogant and often was made fun of as silly
and presumptuous.  (Note:  Although educated, she worked
year after year in a bar.)
      Unsolicited advice:  told to put my hair up in a
bun, use no makeup, wear glasses.  Student commenting
on my "Barbie Doll" voice while working on a group
project.  Instructor's negative comments on oral report.
Women as well as men:  At least men have the excuse of
being conditioned to react sexually to women who sound
and act "feminine."
      Unfair focus on appearance:  Brunettes are more
likely to be taken seriously?
```

Norman Mailer on Marilyn Monroe in <u>Marilyn</u>: "She was not the dark contract of the passionate brunette depths that speak of blood, vows taken for life, and the furies of vengeance . . . no, Marilyn suggested sex might be difficult or dangerous with others, but ice cream with her." (p. 15) "So we think of Marilyn who was every man's love affair . . . who was blonde and beautiful and had a sweet little rinky-dink of a voice . . . which carried such ripe overtones of erotic excitement and yet was the voice of a little child." (pp. 15-16)

Note: Pitch of the voice is determined by size of the larynx and how tightly the muscles in it are stretched. Voiceprints like fingerprints: can be used for identification.

Writing Sample: First Draft

Dream Girls

The stereotype killed Marilyn Monroe, the blonde bombshell with the sexy voice. Marilyn wanted the role, so she played the game. She became, as Norman Mailer says in <u>Marilyn</u>, "every man's love affair," blonde and beautiful and "with the voice of a little child." As Mailer says, she "suggested sex might be difficult or dangerous with others, but ice cream with her." Marilyn used her looks; she lived a role for the public that her inner self couldn't be, and she died of an overdose.

The stereotype is hard to fight. The idea of the dumb blonde is cut deep into the minds of men, bosses, those in power, other females. A blonde with good looks and a soft musical voice has a steeper climb to the top than her dark-haired sister.

TV perpetuates this idea by creating roles for blonde airheads. In one show, canceled at first because it offended women's groups but then brought back, the public could watch a blonde dream girl in tight sweaters and plastic gloves delight the two men who hired her as a maid. The role of Diane in <u>Cheers</u> was at first coveted by actresses because Diane was college-educated and had some depth to her character. In the end, Diane was a fool. She had an education that made her arrogant and presumptuous. She worked year after year hopping tables in a bar. There are serious roles for blonde women on TV, but the stereotype is hard to shake.

I am blonde. I have a soft musical voice. I have always had high grades. Working as a tutor, I have helped other students improve their work. I have worked as a bookkeeper and assistant personnel manager. Still, there are people who don't take me seriously because of the way I look and sound. I've been told to put my hair up in a bun, wear glasses, quit wearing makeup, and work to lower the pitch of my voice. I want to teach, but I don't want to play a role; I want to be myself.

Men are not the only ones doing the stereotyping. I had a female instructor criticize my voice as unprofessional during an oral report critique. I had a female student say in a group endeavor that I should go last because my "Barbie Doll" voice would leave an emotional impression on the audience.

All blonde hair does not come out of a bottle, and the pitch of the voice is determined by the size of the larynx and by how tightly the muscles in it are stretched. Voiceprints, like fingerprints, are highly individual and can be used as a means of identification.

The myth of the beautiful childlike blonde will probably always exist as long as men want to take care of women who give them pleasure and who need protection. The stereotype will wane when men begin to respect women who take care of themselves.

The Unifying Thesis Everything in the "Dream Girls" paper is relevant to the writer's central idea: The stereotype of the dumb blonde is unfair, ignorant, obsolete. Such a central idea, or thesis, can serve as a powerful unifying device for a paper. If you spell out your thesis early in a paper, your readers have an answer to a very basic question in their minds: What is the point? What are you trying to prove? What are you trying to show? (Sometimes we *lead up* to the central thesis, winding up a paper by saying: "Therefore, we must conclude that....")

How do we push toward a unifying thesis? A genuine thesis is not just a hand-me-down—a secondhand idea or prejudice. It is the result of checking things out, of taking a close look. The thesis unifying the following student paper grew out of much relevant firsthand experience. The writer remembered signing up for a workout program that became a horrendous drain on her pocketbook. She came to know well a woman obsessed with the "model look." The writer vividly remembered the constant stream of ads pushing fitness-related products, but she equally vividly remembered reading articles about the abuses and phobias associated with a fanatic overemphasis on the fitness ideal. Here is a rough chart of how her experience and reading might funnel into a central thesis:

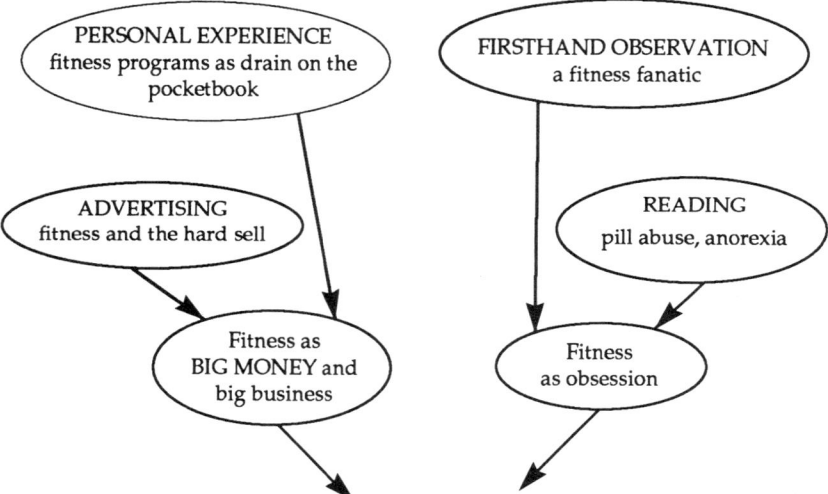

Thesis: In the name of looking good, women everywhere seem to be sacrificing their hard-earned money and jeopardizing their health.

Study the following paper presenting and supporting this thesis. Where and how does the writer present her thesis—how does she lead up to it? In what order does she arrange the supporting material? Where or how does her conclusion echo the original thesis?

Writing Sample: Thesis and Support

The Fitness Drain

The bill for my spa payment came in the mail again this month. Two years ago First Lady Spa promised me that if I would pay them only $21.40 a month for two and one-half years they would let me use their first-class weight lifting machines and that I could attend their endless number of aerobic classes. As I signed the agreement, they handed me a 20% discount card for Leotard World, and I was on my way to perfect fitness. For the first two months I was faithful and dedicated. It seemed, though, that the more I went to the spa, the more items I had to buy. First of all, I needed special aerobic shoes which cost about $35.00. Then I noticed how frayed and boring my work-out gear looked in comparison to that of the other women at the spa. I used my 20% discount card. Then I realized that no one wore the same leotard twice in the same week. But, as my money dwindled, so did my enthusiasm. I realized how much I hated being in the same room with sweaty women swearing at their reflections. I decided to work out at home and have continued to do so erratically ever since.

Although I did receive more encouragement when I was working out at the spa than when I worked out at home, the pat on the back usually consisted of "Hey, you're looking great! Keep it up." Looking great seemed to be the major motivation for working out. In the name of looking good, women everywhere seem to be sacrificing their hard-earned money and jeopardizing their health in an attempt to attain the mirage of superficial perfection.

When I was selling cosmetics I worked with a woman who was absolutely obsessed with her looks. She was determined to become a "body model," and she would enter various swimsuit competitions to gain experience and get publicity. Her appearance was perfect for her to obtain her goals, but the way she went about looking good was dangerous. After working until 9 p.m. she would then go exercise for three hours. What was terrible, though, was that she told me that often when she would come home from exercising, she would black out. Part of the cause of these fainting spells may have been that in her quest for the perfect body, she would hardly ingest anything except diet coke. When she did finally eat something substantial, she would feel guilty and make herself vomit. But, also, surely the intense pressure and strain from working out three hours each night played a major role in her physical problem.

Admittedly, my former co-worker is an extreme example, and there are probably many healthy-looking people who are also healthy inside due to exercise. However, the rise of fitness wizards like Joe Weider prove that this woman's obsessive quest for perfection through fitness and exercise isn't so bizarre.

Joe Weider first gained recognition when he started the Mr. Universe and then the Mr. Olympia body building contests. Weider has developed a financial empire based on the current exercise craze. He now publishes <u>Muscle and Fitness</u> magazine which he uses to sell both his products and his ideas about fitness and exercise. A quick glance through the January issue reveals endless advertisements for Joe Weider's Dynamic Life Essence ($24.95), Joe Weider's Anabolic Mega Paks ($24.95), Joe Weider's Dynamic Body Building Blocks ($16.95), all of which are to be consumed together for maximum results ($66.85 plus tax). There's also Joe Weider's Aerobic Formula ($26.95) that's specially formulated for active women. Women who buy this product will probably do so in hope of looking as good as the woman in the ad who has not only a lovely lavender leotard but also weights that look dyed to match.

We discover the other side of the coin when we read about the abuse of appetite-suppressant pills and about teenagers who become victims of anorexia and bulimia in an attempt to become like the tanned perfect bodies that look at them from the covers of fitness magazines. Instead of working and working out in healthy outdoor surroundings, we look for the secret of perpetual good looks in capsules and machines. In the process, we drain our bank accounts and our energy. The pioneers of the American past would laugh at us.

REVISING: WRITING AND REWRITING

In the real world, even a short memo may go through several rewrites in response to input or feedback from others. For the professional writer, a first draft is a trial run—it gives the writer a chance to see what works well and what needs work. Most published writing has gone through one or more revisions, often with a major change in emphasis or direction.

People who know writing mainly from the point of view of the passive reader often do not realize that the finished product is the result of rewriting and second thoughts. Read the following student paper, and then study the student writer's account of how she revised and reshaped the paper in response to peer review and feedback from the instructor.

A Stranger Lives Within Me

For a person with a chronic or terminal illness such as kidney failure, cirrhosis of the liver, or blockage of the arteries, replacement of the diseased organ with a healthy one is becoming an increasingly popular method of treatment. Receiving someone else's organ is a drastic alteration of the physical body and the person's mental condition. Thus, after a transplant, the patient has physical pain and also a difficult psychological adjustment.

Whether the transplanted organ is a cornea or a heart, the process of psychological adjustment is similar in most recipients. Immediately after a successful operation, the recipient experiences feelings of renewed life and heightened self-confidence. Helen Michalisko, a Johns Hopkins University social worker, observes, "There's a sense of rebirth and renewal; like a newborn child, they think everything they see and touch is sensational" (qtd. in Rodgers 63). These feelings result not only from the recipient's exhilaration at being physically "well," but also from the euphoria induced by routine medications (Rodgers 63).

After a short period of time, however, indications of physical rejection or other postoperative complications revive the worries and concerns that the recipient experienced before the transplant. As a result, the patient again becomes frightened, yet at the same time tries to deny any fears of possible death (Rodgers 63).

Later, after release from the hospital, the recipient recognizes the realities of organ transplant, with depressing effects. "If I had known then what I know now, I probably would have declined the surgery," revealed a young man after a heart transplant (Rodgers 60-61). Although he had been cautioned prior to his operation, this patient became depressed by the pain, diet limitations, and constant fear that still remained with him.

The recipient, in effect, experiences stages of acceptance to this new life, including uncertainty, apprehension, and even denial of the alien organ. Like the stages of grief, the recipient must adjust the mental image of the body to include a transplanted organ.

Some recipients, however, cannot learn to accept the alien organ. The self-image and personality of these people are often altered because they feel that another person is living inside them, to the point that some attempt to assume characteristics of the donor. For example, Dr. Donald T. Lunde, a psychiatrist at Stanford University Medical Center, reports a patient who, upon receiving the heart of a prominent citizen, felt a compelling urge to change his life-style and "become more like the donor" (qtd. in Newsweek, 118).

What does all this medical trauma have to do with me? With you? One of us may be next--as donor or recipient. The statistics are beginning to stack the odds so that young persons especially can expect in their lifetimes to be recipients of a transplanted organ. And why not? If medical science continues its phenomenal success, I see no reason why transplants of arms and legs can't occur to join transplants of eyes, hearts, kidneys, and livers.

I look forward to such medical breakthroughs. Therefore, I have filled out my donor card. If I die, at least a part of me lives on. In the same manner, I would accept a donor organ. Granted, I would surely experience the various stages of coping as described above, but I would be alive, thanks to medical science.

Any recipient who can successfully meet the physical and the mental challenges will be able to take full advantage of this miraculous medical achievement and enjoy a greatly improved life.

Works Cited

Rodgers, Joann. "Life on the Cutting Edge." Psychology Today Oct. 1984: 58-67.

"Transplant Psychosis." Newsweek 19 May 1969: 118.

As the instructor said, the student did not write this paper "off the top of her head." Here is the student's account of the three successive drafts she wrote of this paper:

I wrote the first draft after reading a Newsweek article. But my peer reviewer on that draft asked me bluntly, "So what? You report on organ transplants, but you don't make a point. I can't find a thesis."

That's when I developed the ending. For the first time, I confronted the issue myself and addressed the reader more realistically. My whole purpose changed with this new mission of action. I signed a donor card and called on my readers to do the same.

However, my instructor, after looking at the second draft, said I needed some examples or quotations of persons who had experienced donor transplants. I went back to <u>Newsweek</u> to cite some material from that article. While in the library I found another reference in <u>Readers' Guide to Periodical Literature</u>. It turned out to be the good article by Joann Rodgers in <u>Psychology Today</u>. Those two articles gave me the voice of authority on the subject and also provided my answer to the instructor's challenge: to find examples and quotations of people involved.

I had to write this paper three times to get it right, if it really is. My research paper manual helped me write correct citations and a bibliography. I had never realized that little papers like this would require such formal handling. I made an A on it, but I think it needs more development, yet that would make it into a research paper rather than a short essay of explanation.

So that's it. I drafted a report. Then I changed it into a thesis essay. On third draft I added the sources to make it into a little research paper.

—Susan Noe, in *Interactions,* James D. Lester ed.

Each paper is different. Nevertheless, teachers, editors, and reviewers find themselves repeatedly giving similar advice for revision. Here are some possible general guidelines:

- *Aim at a clearer focus.* Of several related or intertwined issues, which one should you really concentrate on? For instance, the student who compiled the reading notes on "English first" is likely to write a first draft in which "English as official language" and "future of bilingual education" are two competing topics. Focusing on the bilingual *student* might make for a stronger paper.

- *Spell out your main point.* Usually writers profit from asking themselves after finishing a first draft: What am I really trying to tell the reader? Often we do some of our real thinking after we have a first rough version of our material down on paper. Sum up and spell out your revised conclusions, incorporating your second thoughts.

- *Push toward real-life examples.* Plug in additional examples or evidence where your ideas might sound like your mere say-so. Make the examples you already have more convincing or dramatic by adding real-life detail.
- *Check the overall flow of ideas.* Sum up your strategy in a few sentences. Could you explain to a reader *why* you present your ideas in their present order? Should you reshuffle sections for a smoother flow of ideas from cause to effect, from problem to solution, or from then to now?
- *Proofread. Proofread again.* If you want your readers to pay attention to your ideas about Greek drama, you cannot afford to misspell *Oedipus* and *tragedy*. You cannot afford to write *immortal* when you mean *immoral*. The right word, correct spelling, and conventional punctuation are basic survival skills for the writer who expects to be taken seriously.

Most writing textbooks and most writing teachers today distinguish between *revision* for effective strategy or adequate support and final *editing* for better word choice, clearer sentences, or less improvised punctuation. But in practice the two overlap. Even while you are strengthening weak links in your argument, you will be attending to mixed metaphors ("standing on the threshold of a new horizon"), clichés ("the cart before the horse"), and mixed clichés ("Rome was not burut in a day"). You will rewrite entangled or roundabout sentences on the Who-does-what? (or Who-kicks-whom?) model: "All job-related disbursements have to be approved by your supervisor prior to expenditure of funds" becomes "Your supervisor has to approve all job-related expenses before you spend the money."

The life cycle of much student writing is prematurely terminated when the paper has been revised and given a grade. Often the paper is filed, or it otherwise disappears from view. With the professional writer, of course, final revision and editing are merely the last two steps toward the payoff: publication. The writer's reward comes when other people care enough to read the finished piece—to be pleased, instructed, provoked, or inspired by it. (Even the reader who quarrels with it or finds fault with it is paying it the compliment of taking it seriously.)

Today, with the resources of desktop publishing and inexpensive photocopying, more and more students see their best writing informally published and circulated. Class publications and school publications (as well as regional and national essay contests) provide the outlet without which writing remains incomplete, like singing to yourself in the mirror. Writing does not become real if we think of it as a message put in a bottle, to be washed up on some distant beach. We write to be read.

Part Two

The Writer's Tasks

We do not learn to write once and for all. There is no one-size-fits-all formula for effective writing. We learn by taking on gradually more demanding tasks. As we go on to a new project, we try to remember and apply what we learned from a previous one. With more extended experience, we are likely to find that some skills and procedures are indeed basic to good writing, regardless of the specific writing situation.

The kinds of writing illustrated in this collection of student writing cover a range of tasks that should be part of a writer's education. These tasks are not totally separate or mutually exclusive; they overlap and combine in much real writing. However, they illustrate some of the more important things that good writers know how to do.

We can sort out familiar writing tasks in different ways, going, for instance, from the most practical (instructions, directions) to the inspirational. The sections that follow proceed in an order that accounts for the structure of many of today's writing courses. You will first read papers that focus on personal experience and self-expression, going on to papers that focus on the world outside us, and moving on to papers that focus on reaching the reader, the audience.

Good writers can articulate their personal thoughts and feelings; they are able to turn to firsthand personal experience to bring abstract ideas and theoretical issues to life. But they also know how to do justice to the world "out there." They are alert observers; they know how to gather and process information. Finally, they are aware of the reader's thoughts and feelings. They know how to help the reader understand; they know how to convince and persuade.

1
Experience: Telling Your Story

What do writers write about? Many write about themselves. Celebrities write about what made them successful and what held them back. The sons and daughters of celebrities write about growing up in the shadow of rich and famous parents. Political leaders or business tycoons write the story of their early struggles, of the thinking that went into major decisions, of major triumphs and disappointments. Many of the books on the shelves of your local bookstore were written by people to unburden themselves, to come to terms with problems or traumas, or to try to understand who and what they are.

Some of the strongest student writing is done by students not intent on impressing or amusing or bamboozling the reader but trying to do an honest stocktaking of their own experience. When you write about yourself, you write on a subject on which you are the foremost expert. You have a chance to take your readers beyond the superficial impressions, stereotypes, or prejudices that keep us from knowing other people.

The following student papers illustrate some of the special strengths of writing based on personal experience.

Home, Sweet Home

One of the most elementary needs of the young is for a place where they are loved and protected. Many people remember nostalgically the golden childhood years when there was "no place like home." What happens to people who do not have those memories of a happy childhood home?

Free at Last

Parents shape and guide us and often try to mold us in their own image. One of the basic archetypal experiences of the adolescent is the gradual and often painful cutting of the cord. Part of growing up is asserting one's own separate identity.

Glamour

One of the great educational experiences for many young people is the first venture into the world of work. Often the realities of the job are different from the glamorous or idealized picture we may have had in our minds.

Burn

On subjects like sex, alcohol, or drugs, young people encounter much propaganda, moralizing, and hypocrisy. This paper presents the honest testimony of someone struggling with addiction and presenting it not as a matter of moral choice but as a matter of "self-preservation."

My Parents, Myself

Writing honestly about one's background often means trying to come to terms with contradictory influences and mixed emotions. This paper sorts out the influence two very different parents had on the writer.

Home, Sweet Home

I seem to be especially vulnerable to the effects of platitudinous sayings about home, such as "Home is where the heart is," or "Home is where you hang your hat," or Dorothy murmuring in The Wizard of Oz, "There's no place like home, there's no place like home, there's no place like home." These nostalgic sentiments stir up surges of sadness and anger in me. I feel like a kid who hasn't been invited to a birthday party and who stands outside the house where the party is in full swing, looking longingly in the windows at the festivities, and yet wanting to run in and burst everybody's balloons with a long, sharp pin. For those of us who live in or come from chaotic or abusive families, the yearning for a home and a feeling of belonging can be very confusing.

When people hang "Home Sweet Home" signs up in their houses, they are responding to a need for a place in which they can feel comfortable, and a need for a group of people who understand, accept and love them. For many, home is where Mom or Dad is because that is where they feel loved and accepted and it is an environment that is familiar to them. Like Dorothy in The Wizard of Oz, they long for the warmth and familiarity of home when they leave. As adults they may recreate that home by marrying, having children, and living a life similar to that of their parents. They may visit their parents often, maintaining the warm bonds of belonging and the familiar sense of home.

But what do the people do for whom the familiar is painful? The children of parents who are abusive, neglectful, or absent grow up into adults who feel the same, if not more intense, needs for a comfortable place where they can be themselves and for people who will accept and love them. But if they have never experienced consistent love or felt at ease in the homes in which they lived, they may be bewildered at the task of creating a home for themselves. I spent much of my childhood and adolescence hiding behind my closed bedroom door to avoid facing the unpredictable rages of my mother and the silent disapproval of my father. I remember fantasizing as a teenager of the day I would have my own apartment and the life I would live away from the people I feared and needed. When I finally did move into an apartment of my own, I slept on the floor in a sleeping bag amid unpacked boxes of books and belongings for months. I did not know how to make myself a home and I essentially recreated a feeling of coldness and alienation in my newfound haven of freedom.

Creating a home that is not familiar but is warm can be a difficult challenge for people from unhappy childhood homes. We must, like Dorothy, discover that the answer to our feeling of homelessness lies within us and not over the rainbow. We can refuse to recreate the familiar but painful atmosphere of home and with courage look for the good in the unfamiliar and make it our new home. Long after I unpacked the boxes and hung some pictures on my apartment walls, I was still associating with men and women that reminded me of my parents. It will take time to say good-bye to all that and to open myself up to the unfamiliar.

THE READER'S TURN:

1. What is a platitude? What feelings about home are part of the perennial appeal of *The Wizard of Oz*?

2. Some writers merely tell us *about* their feelings. Others know how to project their feelings into gestures, events, or actions that mirror them or act them out. Which does this paper do—where and how?

3. What kind of person is speaking to you in this paper?
4. If this writer told you her story as to a friend, what would you say?
5. What does the idea of home mean to *you*?

Free at Last

My memories of childhood are dim and hazy as if I lived in a fog or perhaps was only a casual observer in my life. My most vivid memory is not of an event but rather of a feeling which was with me at most of my waking moments. The feeling was that I lacked control of my life and actions. I suppose that all children feel this to some extent or another. The difference in me was that this feeling came not from my being told what to do, but rather from my inferring what my actions were to be and controlling myself to fit this image, all the while hating the restraints which I was placing on myself.

I suppose this bound feeling emanated from the attitudes of my parents. In my earliest memories, I can remember my parents creating an aura of superiority about our family. The actions of others, even relatives, were constantly reviewed, chastised, and condemned. When my aunt's children started getting in trouble with the law, when my cousin got divorced, when our close family friends became heavy drinkers, we secretly judged them and isolated ourselves from them, all the while professing our Christianity. I often participated in this, but gradually I came to resent being separated and elevated above those who did not live up to our standards. Still it was hard to isolate myself from this indoctrination, and more often than not, I would censor my own actions so as to live up to the ideals of my parents. In retrospect the events often seem small and petty but at the time they were enormous and life-shattering. I can remember once, as a junior in high school, I lied to my parents about the movie I was going to see. I wanted to see Young Frankenstein, a very popular "R" rated movie, but I told them I was going to see Jeremiah Johnson, which was rated "G". I can still feel the guilt of slinking out the door to taste the forbidden fruit. There was a feeling that someone else's will was being superimposed upon my own.

This feeling of guilt also affected me in other ways. I did things not because I wanted to, but because I felt it was expected of me. I went out for the football team even though I had no desire to play, and for three years I sat on the bench, finally earning a varsity letter because I was a senior, not because I was a good player. I joined the Air Force J.R.O.T.C. because my dad had been an Air Force pilot and I knew that was what he wanted. I did what my parents wanted, believed what my parents believed. I did not exist; the model child which my parents had created was merely borrowing my shoes.

By the end of my senior year, things had reached an unbearable level. I had won an R.O.T.C. scholarship to the state university, another attempt to prove my sterling character. But it was clear that something was changing. I had attempted to pay rent while staying at home so as to gain some little freedom and ended up poorer but with no more freedom. One evening after we had finished dinner, my parents fell asleep in front of the television. I left the living room, with my parents snoring and M*A*S*H still playing, to go hang out with my friends. Time passed quickly, as it does when spent idly, and before I knew it, it was well after midnight. I was unsure what to do, but I decided to try and sneak back in the house. As I crept past the living room windows, I peered in trying to see if anyone was awake. Suddenly, I was blinded by a light. My mother had been sitting on the couch in the darkness waiting for me to return home. She pointed towards the door, gesturing for me to come inside. My mom and dad both questioned me for what seemed hours asking where I was, what I was doing, and who I was with.

I did not know it at the time, but the scholarship was to become my escape route. Through it I was able to glimpse the freedom I so badly needed. Once I had enrolled at the university, I no longer had to worry about the watchful eye of my parents. That is not to say that they did not try to control my behavior. There were countless conversations about whom I associated with, how often I studied, and how much beer I drank. But a phone call across five hundred miles has little power to discern the truth. Finally I could experiment with the freedom which had so long eluded me. I skipped classes. I drank till I fell down. I experimented with smoking pot.

This sounds as if I slipped into this new lifestyle quite easily, but the fact is that I was constantly torn between my desire for freedom and my guilt at experiencing it. I was beginning to feel sorry about my exploits and began discussing my intention to join the priesthood. This sounds rather melodramatic, but it was met with great applause. Fortunately the Jesuits suggested that I spend more time in school, gaining some life experience, before I join the order. My parents continued to call me, trying to keep tabs on my life, but these calls no longer had the same effect on me. I was beginning to feel no guilt about enjoying life.

THE READER'S TURN:

1. What is the keynote or unifying thread of this paper? Where is the keynote first sounded? Where is it echoed or reinforced?
2. What for you is the most striking or revealing incident in this paper?
3. Does the pattern of growing up traced in this paper have a parallel in your own experience? How was your experience similar or different?
4. We naturally see things that happen to us from our point of view. Can you imagine yourself in the parents' shoes? Could you rewrite this story as it would sound if told from the parents' point of view?
5. Write the story of some strong influence in your life that you have tried to fight or that has left you with mixed or contradictory emotions.

Glamour

Everyone knows that the life of a model is glamorous and fun. They get to dress up in expensive, designer clothes, eat out at fancy restaurants with rich, handsome men, and attend all sorts of lavish parties with a wide variety of interesting and affluent people. This is the way most people picture a "typical" model to be. The majority of the general public views models as young, dumb or airheaded, skinny, sexy and beautiful;

generally, someone who wears beautiful, stylish clothes and earns lots of money for doing almost nothing.

And now for a glimpse of reality: It's seven o'clock on a cold winter morning at a secluded beach along the coast of California. There is an icy breeze blowing inland as the remains of a misty fog swirl by. The sun is still rising and it is about thirty degrees outside. Huddled around in a circle are four of America's up and coming top models, all wearing long fur coats and holding steaming, hot cups of coffee as a means of keeping warm. After approximately twenty minutes, when the sun has risen to a photographically ideal position and the photographer has finished setting up his equipment, the models are beckoned to shed their beautiful furs and step out onto the cold, clammy sand wearing nothing but the latest fashions in bikini wear. At this time they are expected to frolic about in a light-hearted, fun-loving fashion while posing for the photographer as if it were a hot summer day. A few minutes prior to shedding their furs, the models are told to rapidly drink down a glass of ice cold water in order to neutralize the warmth of their bodies with the bitter cold ocean air so that their breath will not be visible on film. As you may have noticed, the myths and realities of modeling are quite contrary to each other. The myths can be glamorous, yet the realities can be rather harsh.

Starting out, a model must first find a good agency that is willing to promote her. This can take many hours, days, weeks of pounding the pavement and sending out résumés to potentially interested agencies. Once with an agency, she must learn to walk and climb up and down stairs properly and gracefully. Speaking clearly and intelligently is yet another skill to be learned. It is not always the face and figure that get her the job; quite the contrary, it's what she says and how she says it that counts.

Additional skills that need to be mastered are make-up and wardrobe, both of which require knowing the correct colors for the individual involved. To have a well coordinated wardrobe made up of the best colors, lines, and styles is imperative in order to attain a professional look. Achieving this can be quite costly--

and yet it does not include the cost of professional photographs for a portfolio, which can run up to hundreds of dollars.

Other aspects of the profession include long, sometimes boring hours spent standing around waiting for everything and everybody to be ready to start working. I say "standing around" because that's most of what a model does all day, stand around while wearing clothes that she doesn't own; therefore, she must not get them dirty, not even wrinkled.

The first several jobs of a beginning model are unimpressive and geared toward "gaining experience"; this means that she doesn't get paid. Some of these jobs include mannequin modeling (standing perfectly still for hours at a time), dispersing pamphlets throughout a shopping center for a particular store whose clothes she is modeling, and possibly a few fashion shows (if she is lucky). However, once she starts acquiring paying jobs, the agency receives half of the paycheck.

By this time, the life of a model may not sound so glamorous. There are a lot of rude and egotistical people one must work with, many long hours, low-paying or no-paying jobs, and the frustration of trying to be "perfect" at all times.

It takes will and determination to be a model and to persevere through the harsh realities and the more superficial dimensions of this career.

THE READER'S TURN

1. The contrast between illusion and reality is an age-old topic for writers. How and how well does this paper deal with this familiar theme?

2. What details help give this paper the appeal of the inside story, taking us behind the scenes, telling us things that are thought-provoking or unexpected?

3. What kind of reader do you think would make a good audience for this paper? Do you make a good audience? Why or why not?

4. Write about an experience that made *you* discover the reality behind a glamorous or misleading surface.

Burn

Crank (the street name for methamphetamine), also called poor man's cocaine, is a stimulant. Its main effect is sleep deprivation. Your mind becomes isolated, and internally you imagine your concentration to be incredibly intense. There is a definite rush accompanying the initial dose. The worst is the burn. After the initial effects wear off, and you've lost your first night of sleep, the burn begins. Your gut tightens up; you begin to sweat. Yet through this all is a kind of nervous exhilaration. But in the end fatigue wins out. Depending on how long the run was, it sometimes takes days to feel normal again. Even after ten hours of sleep you still feel tired. Its is a bone-weary kind of tired that has with it a mental sluggishness that sometimes veers into depression. You know the depression is only an effect of the drug and lack of sleep, but the knowledge doesn't help. All subsequent uses merely help maintain an illusion of a status quo, to postpone the inevitable downswing.

One day while at work, having not slept for three days, I was experiencing "brownouts," lapses in concentration. I was using the forklift to pull a two-thousand pound pallet of copy paper off the top shelf fifteen feet in the air when I blanked out. The forks were not all the way into the pallet as I began to pull it from the shelf. It lurched and almost came down on me. Shaken, I went to the bathroom, splashed water on my face. Back in the warehouse, the pallet was still there, leaning dangerously against the forks. The rest of the crew had gone home for the day, and so I was alone. There was no way to bring the pallet down intact. Finally, I jerked the pallet hard with the forklift to straighten it and brought it down, losing about half of the fifty-pound cartons. They fell all around me. Had I not straightened the pallet out, the ton of paper would all have fallen on top of me.

This one incident worked on me like no other. I had been ready to quit for a long time. I knew the damage crank was doing to me mentally. Had the incident happened earlier I would have most likely shrugged it off and done another line. I needed a catalyst to help me make a decision I obviously didn't have the strength of character to make on my own. The worst part was that I actually liked the drug. I liked its effects; I liked the peer approval; there was a ritualistic sense of communion in doing up a couple of grams with my friends. And because no major catastrophe had happened, I had fooled myself into thinking that I was in control. What allowed me to walk away from this addiction was not a moral choice but an instinct of self-preservation.

THE READER'S TURN:

1. Subjects like the one treated in this paper are often hidden in a fog of accusations, self-justification, evasions, or wishful thinking. Is this writer playing games with you as the reader?

2. How is this paper different from what you would expect in a paper about drug abuse?

3. Does this paper confirm or does it change your own thinking on this topic? Why or how?

4. Compare and contrast current rhetoric or propaganda on the subject of drugs with what you have observed at first hand.

5. Write about an event or development that made you realize something important.

My Parents, Myself

Last week I heard the poet Etheridge Knight speak to a group of students and teachers. He said there were only two things he knew for certain in his life, and the rest was all just his opinion. He said he knew who his mother was--and he knew who his father was.

What I have often questioned is whether I am more like one parent than the other. There were two different people inside my father, or so it seemed to me. My early memories of him are positive: He made ships with intricate detail, and he made a butterfly collection of specimens he had caught himself. He took us to the beach. He looked self-assured; he looked strong. He was a tall, slender man who had come from an English middle-class background, and who had bettered himself through higher education. He met my mother while he was going to law school.

She was of pure Irish stock, and very much a working-class girl with a little style or class. Once Joe Dimaggio had sent her a drink from across the bar, or so she said. Though she was short, she had a perfect figure and dressed well on her modest income. She had a pretty smile and baby-fine blonde hair which she always wore in a bun on top of her head. My mother was an only child and her mother died when she was fifteen, leaving her to be cared for by her aunt. At the age of twenty-seven, she married my father, believing in family and hard work and all the prospects a good marriage would bring. They moved to San Francisco at my father's request and rapidly had nine children.

When I was young, I favored my father because his attention was harder won and therefore more desirable. I remember choosing his home state for my sixth grade report. But, as I grew older, I did not want anything to do with him. I was no longer as sweet or as pretty, and he was no longer as kind or as safe. I resented his rules--his strict attention to "form." We were expected to dress before coming downstairs in the morning; we were expected to say good night to our father, even if he was passed out in his chair. As a young adult in my teens, I felt as if I could never do anything right. For instance, I could never remember how to set a table properly. More importantly, I could not choose the "right" vocation. I wanted to be an artist, and he did not have the confidence that I would succeed.

As an adult, I understand why I despaired so much of becoming like him. I understand his failures in the light of my mother's success. He shut people out of his life. He was a loner and he became an alcoholic, a word I did not know the meaning of until I was twenty-five. I can remember sitting in the half-lit kitchen waiting for my mom to come home from work. Earlier in the evening, my father had come back from Thrifty's as he always did on the weekends, with soda and potato chips for us kids, and a bottle for himself. He would empty the bag on the counter, putting his beer in the refrigerator, and carrying his bourbon to the den. I would sit on the stool and wait to watch his tall figure stumble towards the bathroom and complain about this or that.

People always moved toward my mother. I remember working with her at the Pacific Telephone Company, and watching the women she worked with treat her with respect and affection. Some girls called her "Mom," which pained me very much. Though I was like my father, I wanted my mother's closeness. When she died there were hundreds of people at her funeral. When my father died there were only a dozen people--men he had worked with and a few neighbors that had never known him well.

I remember the Christmas days that followed my mother's death and how my father tried to manage. I came to know who he was with some clarity three months before he died. I see him lacing red and green ribbons through the chandelier that hung over the dining room table, and putting out dishes of candy for us kids. I see him standing in the living room looking around at us, attempting a few pleasant comments, and then retreating awkwardly to his den where he sat with his books and the red curtains that hung down from the tall windows, putting coal into the fire because it was cheaper than wood.

My mother was so different. She lacked pretenses and did not expect life to give her a lot. She gave to life instead. She gave her time to the infants at the Sunday school. She gave her home to a young girl of my own age when that girl's mother could give her neither a home nor a family. She gave her home to a young man she met in an English class who was drifting. My father did not know how to gather life towards him.

I have often feared not finding my mother's goodness inside myself. I have fought off the separateness my father carried inside himself, his failures, and his reserve which people see in me and mistake for calm. I loved them both very much.

THE READER'S TURN:

1. We sometimes read papers that dutifully pay tribute to parents or teachers. How is this paper different?

2. What key details would you include in short capsule portraits of the two people who play the central roles in this paper?

3. This paper traces some slow long-range changes in the writer's thinking and understanding. What are the major stages or waystations?

4. How would you sum the conflicting or contradictory influence the parents had on the writer? How did the influence of the parents help shape the writer's personality?

5. Write about different or conflicting influences in your own life.

WRITING TOPICS 1

What do people write about when they write about themselves? To judge from the amount of autobiographical and biographical writing published, readers have an endless curiosity about other people's lives. What could you focus on that would get your readers' attention or arouse their sympathy? See if any of the following headings activate memories or make you think.

1. Turning Points: We sometimes reach a turning point in our lives after which things are never quite the same. We reach an important waystation in our lives, and looking back later, we can see how it has made a difference. The turning point might be a move away from familiar surroundings, the breakup of a family, a brush with serious illness, the aftermath of an accident, a first experience with crime.

2. Roles: People who take a job that requires them to put on a uniform (of a waitress, nurse, army private, or whatever) know that they are expected to play a role. Other roles don't require a uniform but also make us adopt an expected pattern of behavior: model student, tough kid on the block, Mr. popularity, aspiring star athlete. Sometimes we slide into the adopted role easily; sometimes there is a real gap between the role and the "real you."

3. Roots: Looking back, people often realize that something in their past has had a lasting influence on how they think and feel—on what they hope for and what they are afraid of. For instance, people are likely to be permanently influenced by growing up in a very religious household, in the shadow of a domineering brother or sister, or in a very rich or very poor family. What major influence in you own past helped shape your outlook or your personality?

4. Conflict: In much great autobiography, things turn dramatic when a conflict erupts between opposed loyalties or different points of view. Have you ever felt torn between the conflicting claims of very different friends, of very different parents, or of home and school? Have you ever rebelled against a model or a stereotype that made you say: "That's not who I am"?

5. Learning: Cynics define our human species as the animal that doesn't learn from experience. But often we do feel that we have learned something from what we have witnessed or undergone. Often writing about an experience helps us understand it better or come to terms with it. You might want to write about how you found out what it means to be a woman, a man, an outsider, an immigrant, or an immigrant's child. You might write about how you learned what it means to be a parent, the oldest child, or a close relative of someone in serious trouble.

2
Observation: The Closer Look

Good writers are alert observers. They are not satisfied with a blurry general impression; they move in for a closer look. They know how to bring places and people to life for us by seizing on striking, revealing details. They use the right words to recreate for us the sights and sounds of the landscapes and cityscapes in which we live.

Honest observation does justice to what is "out there." But at the same time we know that we are looking at the world out there through the writer's eye, from the writer's *point of view*. Study the different perspectives from which the writers of the following student papers look at the places and happenings they describe.

The Song and the Dance

Readers exposed to too much grim realism get depressed. This writer recreates for us scenes from the kind of idyllic childhood that many of us wish we had had.

Fourth of July

Travel in general is educational (and a trip to the big city often especially so). This writer makes us look at the dark underside of the city through the wide open eyes of the innocent observer.

The Fire Seeder

Descriptions of our national parks often have a static picture postcard quality (and they often use too many clichés about the unspoilt pristine beauty of Mother Nature). This writer takes us along on an unforgettable dramatic trip through a national park in flames.

What Is Wrong?

We often look at other cultures through the lens of either narrow prejudice or liberal good will and good intentions. This writer, a student who came to this country from Japan, gives us an inside look at the pressure cooker that is the life of the Japanese student.

The Song and the Dance

I am a country girl. I was raised on a small cattle ranch. My mother was a rich city girl, cultured and educated. My father was the son of a North Dakota potato farmer. How they ever found each other I shall never understand. They bought land in Potter Valley, population less than 300, raised four kids, and had a great time living on the land.

Since we lived so far out in the country, our only friends were our animals and each other. My oldest sister, Timothy, was an only child for five years and had to entertain herself a lot of the time. When she was still very young, she began making up dances and plays which she would perform for my parents. When the rest of us came to the age when we could walk and talk a little, we joined the drama. At night our house was like a carnival, with little people running around in costumes, doing tricks, singing and dancing.

Holly, second oldest in age, greatly admired Timothy's dances and often tried to imitate her, unsuccessfully, though. Eventually Holly discovered that she loved to sing. Everywhere she went, a song could be heard--out in the barn, or in the kitchen when she was making jam.

Fred, who is a year older than I, always tried to do everything with my father. He had two jobs on the ranch that he took very seriously when he was little. Whether it was rain or shine, he always fed the dogs and watered them. His other responsibility was his pigs. He had a certain kind of affection for those pigs that I could never understand. He would ride around in the pit on their backs, pull their tails and pat them as if they were kittens.

Our house was sturdy but also beautiful. On the long planked porch sat the green firewood drying. Passing through the great wooden door, we stepped onto a stone floor where wet, muddy boots were kicked off. A woodstove sat at the right giving off delicious heat to cold red fingers. There was always a black coffee pot brewing on the burner. In the center of this kitchen-and-living-room, a brick fireplace stretched up to the ceiling. On winter days, my brother and I would ride our rusty tricycles around it, laughing hysterically. There was a large window which looked down upon the white barn, a horse corral, and rows of berry bushes.

My mother, coming from a big city herself, often worried that we were too sheltered from the outside world and would try to take us to the nearest city as often as possible. It was quite something for her to take four little country bumpkins to a place they never dreamed existed. There were so many strange people to stare at-- the wrinkled old lady with the fur coat and alligator purse, the blind man with the dog, and store clerks with their brisk airs and fast movements.

One of the most exciting times of the year was branding time. My father would get up at daybreak before it was light outside. After he had saddled his mare, Ebony, he would ride up to the house where my mother waited with a thermos of hot coffee to send him off for the day. In the afternoon, while we were swinging under the big oak tree or playing hide-and-seek in the hayloft, we would begin to hear a low roar of feet. We would race to sit in some inconspicuous spot so as not to spook the herd. They tumbled down the hills and squeezed through the gates, the dogs keeping them in a mass. My father came behind riding tall in his saddle.

All of these experiences along with many others helped to shape the person I am now. To be able to sit on a hillside and watch a colt prance in the wind is something which a person does not easily forget. For many years to come, I will still think of the wind, the pigs, and the song and the dance.

THE READER'S TURN:

1. It is one thing for writers to tell us that they have happy childhood memories and another to make those memories real for us as readers. What details help bring these childhood scenes to life for you?

2. A famous French actress called her autobiography *Nostalgia Isn't What It Used to Be*. What for you are the meanings and associations of the term *nostalgia*? What examples from this paper could help you define the term?

3. Who would make a good audience for this paper? Do you? Would the ideal reader have to be someone who grew up in the country?

4. Do you think this paper paints a too idyllic or idealized picture?

5. If you could go on a true nostalgia trip, where would it take you?

Fourth of July

On the Fourth of July, 1986, I was in New York City, specifically downtown and in Greenwich Village. The city was really alive as the day's festivities were getting under way. It was very hot and humid, a day when your clothes melt onto your body. Downtown streets were closed to traffic, so the multitudes of people swarmed in the streets. Vendors shouted about, trying to sell tee shirts and green foam crowns. The streets in the Village were also busy. People were sitting on fire escapes, while others sat on stoops or at cafe tables. There was a strange quiet as the traffic and its usual honking horns and screaming brakes were absent. Only a rare siren and a few street musicians were audible.

The general crowd downtown was basically a mob of families, friends, and sightseers. But up in Greenwich Village the people became a bit more visible. Washington Square was crowded with its normal leather-clad punks and skins, plus the oddly assorted stragglers looking for some place to be seen. A few bag ladies were searching trash cans and bearded men were lying on a patch of lawn with bottle in hand. The person who had a large effect on me was a girl in a total punk dress. She was quite tall and while not what I would call fat, she seemed large. She had her head shaved on the sides with a very thin mohawk which probably measured about ten inches in height. It was a very hot day but she was in heavy black leather pants and jacket, just the same as other days I had seen her there.

Since it was the Fourth of July, I was feeling very patriotic and proud to be in this great country. I had stood in Battery Park looking out at the Statue of Liberty. I was in the city that I loved so much. Sure it has problems, but there was nowhere else I would have rather been. I loved going to the Village for lunch or for a shopping spree away from Bloomies and Macys. I loved being around the unique people who hung out under the Washington Arch. I admit I always had a somewhat romantic notion of the punks. But it only took a glimpse of the real life of one person there to open my mind to a grim reality.

What took place that day in the public restroom in Washington Square did what no article or documentary ever could. As I had little other option, I headed for the restroom which I had never been in before. The room was hot and sticky. Water and trash covered the floor. Several of the stalls had no door on them. I waited for one that did. In the stall on my right there was a girl who was vomiting. The odor was horrid. Her moaning was drowned out by two other girls who were shouting obscenities at one another. I was almost afraid to come out of my stall. When I did, I walked out to a sight I had not been prepared for. The stall across from mine was doorless. In it was the girl with the mohawk I had seen so often. Her jacket was off now. She had a strip of cloth tied around her upper arm. I stood and watched as she put a needle into her arm and shot it full of heroin. She withdrew the needle and took notice of me. Her eyes looked empty. I felt empty.

Here was the birthday of our great nation—a place where everyone was free. But was that girl free? Or was she a slave to a gross power? My eyes opened that day. Until then I had not seen the hard, cold reality that was out there. There was nothing romantic about this "rebel" girl. It is painful to look back on how naive I had been. Never again would I see the place or people in the same way.

THE READER'S TURN:

1. How does this writer set the scene? Early in the paper, what are authentic touches showing that the writer "was there"?
2. An alert observer looks beyond the surface. How does this paper act out the classic pattern of going from a naive surface impression to the underlying "grim reality"?
3. What is the special meaning or impact of the title?
4. How do you react to this paper? Do you prefer Romanticism or grim reality?
5. Could you write an exposé of the shabby reality behind the deceptive façade? What would be your subject?

The Fire Seeder

As we drove along the west shore of Yellowstone Lake on our way to dinner, we could see the island in the middle of the lake to our right, its angular shape paralleling our own approach to the inn at the foot of the lake. We watched one lodgepole pine after another turn into a flaming orange-red torch, shooting skyward through the island's black smoke like a fireworks display on a foggy night in San Francisco. The fire swept through the island leaving much of it unscathed before it ran pell-mell into the lake, drawing its last destructive breath in a billowing gasp of steam and black smoke.

We had entered the "burn area" mid-afternoon in the general area of Grant Village. A park attendant flagged us down, told us to turn on our lights and not to stop for any pictures. About two miles down the road, the first fumes of smoke filled our nostrils, irritated our eyes, and besmudged what had been a beautiful blue sky. Around a bend, we encountered the result of the fire's frenetic activity several hours earlier, its erratic path and shape reminding me of a giant baker run amuck with a cookie cutter. Gray ash covered the burnt-out patches of forest, and red-hot coals smouldered in the "snags," the smoking stumps that had once been towering, majestic lodgepole pines.

It was a trip we'd planned for the past year. When the great fire broke out in July, I immediately forecast that the Yellowstone trip would be called off, and the media had a field day. Both the local and national television stations covered its daily progress with dramatic videos that captured both its destructive force and its devastating aftermath in living color. I was delighted, therefore, to hear the evening we arrived in Casper that "Yes, we were going to make the swing through the park" after all, and "Yes, we were going to leave first thing in the morning." This was Thursday evening, August 4th.

We spent Friday afternoon browsing through the marvelous collections of western art and Indian artifacts in the Buffalo Bill Cody Museum in Cody, Wyoming, attended a rodeo that night, and entered Yellowstone Park's east entrance on Saturday morning, August 5th. As we drove through Yellowstone across the north end of Yellowstone Lake to the "Fishing Bridge," the lodgepole pines everywhere caught my attention. With their limbs wrapped around each other, they made a canopy so thick that for miles all I could see were lodgepole pines set onto a surreal landscape, their deceased members creating beautiful artistic forms as they cluttered the barren forest floor. At those times when the road wound out of the forest and into a clearing, we could see smoke rising from the top of another forest grove far in the distance, a part of the more than nine-tenths of Yellowstone which is wilderness and can only be reached on foot or on horseback.

 I was unfamiliar with the park's "natural burn" policy. This policy has been in effect for sixteen years and allows fires caused by lightning to burn themselves out, except where they threaten towns or park buildings. During our swing through the park, fire had already destroyed 15,000 acres. Before it ended, however, the inferno had raged over half of Yellowstone's 2.2 million acres and cost more than $100 million to fight and clean up. The logging industries and the tourist industries, incensed over the park's "natural burn" policy, started their own political firestorm: Wyoming's U.S. Senators called for the resignation of the head of the Park Service. The logging industries wanted to reforest the burned areas to give wooded areas in Yellowstone a "five-year jump" on natural regrowth of the woods and to "get it green again," according to Willamette Industries' general manager for Western timber logging operations. The tourist industry suffered enormous losses because of the fire's adverse publicity. In an average year, 2.5 million tourists visit the park. In August, with fires out of control, the tourist trade was off 30% according to published reports. When the fire finally subsided, public opinion seemed to be questioning a policy that could allow such a degree of devastation and destruction to Yellowstone Park, our oldest national park and the largest wildlife preserve in the United States.

 But as the fire subsided, as the media and television turned their eyes toward more immediate "fires," a calm and rational voice could be heard soothing the public's fears about one of its national treasures. In his article in The Wall Street Journal entitled "Back to Life: Yellowstone Park Begins Its Renewal," Scott McMurray interviewed Research Biologist Donald Despain, who teaches us all an invaluable lesson about ecosystems and the lodgepole pine's regenerative role in the forest's rebirth. Their tiny quarter-inch seeds, or "wings" as Despain calls them, are slowly released from rock-hard pine cones only after the cones have been seared by the passing flames; they require a fire to propagate themselves. The little wings act like the rotary blades of a helicopter in dispersing the seeds which, according to Despain's count, "works out to one million seeds an acre." The burnt "snags," as the charred tree trunks are called, vary in age from a relatively young Civil War period fire to the lodgepole stands that burned this summer which were 250 to 400 years old. According to Despain, it is no coincidence that most burnt trees here were senior citizens and susceptible to fire. As they age, they lose their natural resistance to disease and insects. Dead trees fall to the forest floor, joined by others blown over by the strong winds howling down from surrounding peaks. The thinning canopy, in turn, lets in more light to the forest floor, dormant grass and shrub seeds fill in the open spaces between the trees; the ground clutter thickens; more trees fall; and, with the help of a prolonged drought, "the old forest creates its own funeral pyre."

As John Varley, Yellowstone's chief of research said, "We see what's going on here not as devastation and destruction, but rather, rebirth and renewal of these ecosystems."

THE READER'S TURN:

1. Psychologists talk about "flashbulb memories." These are striking images or memorable scenes that were imprinted on our memories and that we can recall years after in vivid detail. What details in this paper are especially striking or vivid? Which did most to take you to the scene?

2. The writer turned what might have been a static picture postcard view into a live, dramatic experience. How?

3. For the writer, the trip to the park became at the same time an intellectual journey, as writer and reader are made to think about an issue and reach a new and different conclusion. What did the writer learn and how?

4. What questions would you like to ask the writer? Do you approve of the "natural burn" policy? Why or why not?

5. For what current issue could you supply a thought-provoking eyewitness report?

What Is Wrong?

I'm going to write about my terrible period, which was before I decided to come to America. You will see some typical Japanese youngsters' ways of thinking and behaving in this writing. Every Japanese student who wants to go to a university has to take big examinations at the end of winter. My friend and I were going to go to a university, so we studied the same as others at that time.

Shuichi, who was my friend in Japan, was a typical Japanese high school student. He also wanted to go to a public university. I sometimes went to his room to study together, and usually I left my house in the middle of the night because we felt better studying together then. So I told my parents that I was going to go to my friend's house, or sometimes I didn't tell them. I was used to riding my bicycle. We couldn't drive motorcycles or cars, because Japanese have to be 18 years old or more to get a driver's license and 16 to get a motorcycle license, but some high schools like ours didn't allow us to get them. I was stopped several times by the police on the road, and they asked me, "Where are you going at midnight?" Students couldn't go around in the middle of the night, and usually Japanese police were patrolling around the town. I hated them because they made me nervous. When I was stopped by them, every time I had to say, "I am going to my friend's house to study. What's wrong?"

I used to feel good when I arrived at his room. When we were studying in his room, his mother sometimes brought some coffee and sweets for us. The following sentences are typical Japanese conversation between a mother and students. I would say, "Good evening, ma'am. I'm sorry to be bothering you, coming to your house at night." The mother would say, "You are a very hard worker, right? You are good enough to go to the university, but my son can't, you know."

Japanese parents usually say good things about other children but not about their own. Shuichi's mother occasionally came to the room and said, "Please take care of my son. You're intelligent, but my son is stupid." My friend always said, "Shut up, ma'am, and get out of here!" But these were jokes between them. I was always laughing at it.

One night I couldn't go home because it was too cold outside. That night we were arguing about comics we had read in our childhood; we were more excited talking about that than our studies. At last we were competing in how many stories we remembered and neither of us wanted to lose. Neither of us cared about our scores or grades in school.

In the morning, we got up together and prepared to go to school in a hurry. I usually ate breakfast, but he didn't. Even though we were so busy, he was brushing and spraying his hair again and again and was looking at a mirror many times to check it. He said, "This is an important routine for men, isn't it?" We had to wear uniforms and a school hat and school shoes. We didn't have any chance to show our sense of fashion, so some of us attempted to try it on our hair style instead. But there were also a lot of strict rules for hairstyles. However, I was an outlaw; I got a perm in a barbershop. This was completely against our school's rules, so I got a permit which showed my hair was naturally curly hair. When students have such a permit, teachers can't say anything. So I went to get the paper even though some teachers doubted me. But I beat the system; afterwards, I had to go to the barbershop every three months to get a perm; I couldn't show my real straight hair. This sounds crazy now.

After school we had extra classes for studying for the big test. It was six or seven o'clock when we arrived home. For the next hour or so we ate dinner and took a bath and then headed directly for the desk. Sometimes we had a conversation with our family while eating dinner and watching TV. Sometimes it was just a few words. During that terrible period there was no way we could have a lover. We could never think about anything but studying for the test. Friends became unfriendly, and we stopped laughing. Our teachers said, "It's too long to sleep four or five hours every night. If you want to pass the test, you can't sleep more than three hours." We believed that, and it's true.

I guess we have different ways to live. We all have different characteristics which depend on each person. A lot of students are confused as to what their true happiness is. Nobody tells us about happiness, but they give us rules. Do they think we can have real hope without understanding what our happiness is? I am trying to find my happiness and my own self-worth. What's wrong with that?

THE READER'S TURN:

1. When Americans travel abroad, they look at foreign cultures as someone from the outside looking in. Often outsiders fail to understand what is going on—or are told only what the insiders want them to know. What are some striking details that show this to be an inside story rather than an outsider's account?

2. How foreign are foreign cultures to us? What to you is different or strange about the Japanese lifestyle that this student left behind?

3. How does this paper counteract (or confirm) any stereotypes you are aware of about the Japanese?

4. We are often told that under culturally conditioned differences we should look for our common humanity. What in this paper do you think American teenagers can relate to or understand?

5. What inside story do you have to tell?

WRITING TOPICS 2

How good an observer are you? Some people go through life with blinkers, seeing only the car in front of them on the highway or the back of the head of the student sitting in front of them in class. Others notice things; they are forever saying: "Look at that!" People who notice things, who are alert observers, usually have more to say than people who live in their own private cocoons. Which of the following topics would give you a chance to show how good you are at taking in sights and sounds?

1. Cityscapes: City dwellers spend much of their time deploring or defending the city in which they live, or work, or go to school. Suppose you had visitors from out of town. Where would you take them? What would you show them to give them a feeling of what it is like to live here?

2. Journeys: Travel writers delight in taking us to marvelous places as yet undiscovered by tourists or Club Med. But sometimes there are undiscovered places just a few miles from where we live: mudflats, foothills, a deteriorating waterfront, a once fashionable but now shunned park, an ethnic neighborhood. Scout such a place for your readers; take them on a journey there.

3. Back to Nature: Nature writers try to make us cherish the threatened natural world around us. Try to alert your readers to the natural world through the eyes of a bird watcher, beachwalker, rock climber, whale watcher, aquarium buff, or inveterate hiker. What does such a person take in that the blasé ordinary person overlooks?

4. Institutions: We spend much of our lives "institutionalized" in schools or regimented workplaces—and many of us at some point "do time" in camps, army barracks, hospitals, or (God forbid) jails. Recreate in loving detail the prevailing mood or atmosphere of one such place. Write as the insider initiating the outsider.

5. Beyond the Cliché: Life is not a picture postcard, and reality is often different from a Chamber of Commerce brochure. Conduct an unofficial insider's trip to a site, monument, or tourist attraction. Go beyond the cliché—write for readers who do not like official tours or purple prose.

3
Exposition: Let Me Explain

One of the most basic skills of a successful writer is to take in information and ideas and lay them out in a pattern that the reader can follow. We call writing whose main purpose is to lay out information and ideas exposition. Exposition is a large umbrella heading for writing that reports, informs, explains, or instructs. On subjects on which we are ignorant, confused, or stymied, we welcome (or should welcome) writing that sheds light. The reward of the expository writer comes when readers say to themselves: "Now I see!"

The following student papers illustrate some of the major organizing strategies writers use to lay out material in informative writing:

Tree Cutting, Country Style

When we are faced with a difficult task, we welcome clear step-by-step instructions or directions. We appreciate the contribution of a writer who can initiate the newcomer or outsider into a difficult process. This paper on how to take down a tree explains the reasons or benefits, the wherewithal, and the major stages of the procedure.

Life in the Country

Whether to live in the city or in the country has been a favorite topic for writers for at least two thousand years. The writer of this paper revisits the contrast between city and country to justify her own choice and perhaps to help guide ours.

Wolves Mate for Life—Do You?

What are the differences between the old-fashioned traditional marriage and the modern kind? This systematic point-by-point comparison is designed to make us reconsider familiar modern attitudes and assumptions.

And in This Corner!

Sometimes an old familiar scheme of classification proves serviceable for helping us find our way. This writer helps us find our way through the world of sports by sorting them out into upper-class, middle-class, and lower-class events.

65

"Bang! Zap! and Pow!": Punk in Retrospect

When we move into new or unfamiliar territory, we may have to set up our own system of classification to do justice to what we find. This writer tries to set up major stages in the history of punk to help explain his own standards and preferences in the realm of popular music.

Tree Cutting, Country Style

<u>This paper is dedicated to Jessie Strong, a man (then) in his seventies, who taught me everything I know about cutting down a tree.</u>

In the rural Midwest, a good store of firewood is a necessity; many people burn wood as the sole or at least major source of heat for winters with temperatures that may get down well below zero. Some people buy their wood from backwoods folk who cut and sell wood for a living; others, like me, prefer to cut their own wood. This paper describes the usual tree-cutting process under some rather unusual circumstances.

It was a few months after I moved to south central Missouri that during a vicious storm one of two huge oaks in our front yard was struck by lightning. Although it was spring, the leaves gradually turned brown and fell off. The next spring, we hoped to see some sign of life, but there was none. One day Jessie, my neighbor, hollered from where he was sitting on the front porch, "That tree needs to come down!" This I knew only too well.

"When?" I hollered back to Jessie.

"Tomorrow!"

"O.K. About nine? Bring Old Gappy."

Old Gappy was Jessie's six-foot, two-man (or two-woman) cross-cut saw. That saw, with jagged-tooth edge (some teeth three to four inches deep) had cut down many a tree since Jessie had gotten it thirty or so years previously. Unless one has access to a heavy-duty, long-bladed chain saw, a cross-cut saw such as Old Gappy is the main tool needed for a large tree-cutting operation. One also needs a splitting maul (a thicker and blunter version of the traditional ax with a "maul" head--about six to nine pounds of iron at the end of a sturdy hickory handle), a large iron wedge, and a traditional ax as well as a Carborundum sharpening file. For this job, Jessie also brought a thick rope to guide the fall.

Before cutting down a tree, it is always a good idea to notch it in the direction where it is intended to fall. True to form, before we started, Jessie took the Carborundum file, placed it flat against one side of the ax, and gave the blade a few smooth strong outward thrusts to sharpen it--first one side, then the other. Then he took the sharpened ax and cut a wedge-shaped chip out of the trunk on the side where we wanted the tree to fall. First he cut downward at about a 45 degree angle to begin a notch approximately six inches deep into the three foot (diameter) trunk; he then cut straight at a 90 degree angle into the tree to meet the diagonal cut.

After the tree had been notched, Jessie and I each took an end of Old Gappy, grabbed ahold of the sturdy, peg-shaped handles, and set the saw teeth against the trunk, opposite where the chip had been removed. It took a moment of rocking side to side before we stopped forcing and started guiding the blade. Slowly we established the familiar give-and-take movement necessary to a successful tree cutting operation. The two cutters must synchronize their work, surrendering to the steady, common, almost metronomic back-and-forth rhythm of the task. The whole body needs to be taken over by the rhythm, rather than just one's arms. (Using only one's arms, one tires soon.)

It is crucial to learn to let the *saw* do the work of cutting--guide rather than force the saw blade into the wood. If one forces the teeth, even the slightest bit, into the wood, the blade will snag and stop, immovable, in the trunk.

About two-thirds of the way cutting through the trunk, we stopped to tie the rope around the trunk a foot or so higher than we were sawing. I laid the wedge and maul closer to the trunk so they could be handy to grab and use when necessary. Once the rope was securely tied, we resumed sawing.

Soon the tree gave the first slight warning crack. Sometimes, when one gets this close to cutting through the tree, the trunk twists slightly, pinching the saw. In this event, one must pick up the iron wedge, place it, point first, at a 90 degree angle directly behind the blade, and pound it in with the splitting maul until the weight of the tree is eased off the blade and one can proceed to saw. It usually doesn't take much more sawing before, with a final, large c-r-r-r-a-a-a-c-c-k-k-k! the tree leans and then falls.

Many people are terrified to be near a falling tree. The tendency is to panic and run from the tree fall. It's important, therefore, to realize that the safest place to stand is right next to the trunk; one can then step a couple of feet around the trunk in whatever direction is necessary to get out of the way of the tree.

As our tree slowly began to fall, Jessie took ahold of the rope and gently guided the tree to one side, and it fell right on target in the middle of the driveway. What satisfaction to have the job done!

Now that the tree was down, it only remained to cut it into firewood. Another neighbor helped, and in less than three hours, the three of us had the tree cut up and toted to the woodpile near the house. Throughout the next winter, thanks, in part, to that lightning-struck oak, I had plenty of wood to burn for heat.

THE READER'S TURN:

1. When asked to read something not related to their own interests or needs, readers might say "Why bother?" or "Who cares?" Do you make a good audience for this paper? Why or why not?

2. Good workers respect their tools. What does this writer tell you about the necessary tools and preparations?

3. How clear do the major stages of the process become to you?

4. Often an essential part of directions or instructions is warnings about what might go wrong. Does this writer include warnings of this sort?

5. Do you remember an experience that taught you how something works? Share your learning experience with your readers.

Life in the Country

We Americans have come to associate country life with everything that's wholesome. We believe that country life is slow-paced and simple and full of good times and good feelings. Advertising agencies constantly capitalize on this folklore. They sell us everything from cars to cigarettes by placing their products in pastoral settings. They know we're suckers for cowboys and mountains. Most of us are rural romantics, but this nostalgic idealized view of rural life is not consistent with reality.

I've met several young couples who dream of escaping the fast-paced urban lifestyle. They're tired of fighting their way to destinations on crowded highways. They're tired of fighting for parking spaces when they get there. They're tired of the noise, the constant noise. They're tired of driving fast, walking fast, talking fast, playing fast. They're really tired of worrying about their children, feeling isolated in the midst of a large population, and feeling threatened by the high odds of becoming victims of crime. They dream of living in the country where life is easy and good.

I'm a reverse migrant. I grew up in Idaho in a rural community. My parents, grandparents, my brother and his wife, all my in-laws, and my aunts and uncles and cousins galore live there still. I've watched as the meat-packing plant my father and brother and nearly a hundred other men worked for went bankrupt and closed down. I've watched, for years, while my parents have tried to sell their land. Their acreage is worth less now, nearly fifteen years after they bought it, than they paid for it. I've spent hours talking to my sister-in-law about the run of dead-end jobs her husband has had, about their frustration with feeling stuck, about their lack of hope and fear of the future. Country life is not all good times and good feelings. In reality, more and more of the people who live in rural areas are out of work.

While certain urbanites strike out in search of space and quality in living, certain rural dwellers head for the city. Both are looking for an improved quality of life. City kids ride tricycles on litter-strewn sidewalks, play ball on asphalt-paved parking lots surrounded by tall apartment buildings, and stand in line in crowded parks to slide on slides or swing on swings. All this happens while a grown-up watches for safety's sake.

Children do need to breathe clean and smoke-free air, they do need to be safe and have room to play, and they do need to be surrounded by natural, living things. Overall- or jean-clad children in the country, making forts in haystacks and mazes in tall over-the-head weeds, running in open pastures, riding horses, feeding chickens and cattle and sheep, are certainly in touch with living things.

These children can often play for hours safely without adult supervision; therefore, the rural environment does seem to be better suited to the rearing of children.

However, studies show that children raised in rural areas often suffer from economic, social, and educational deprivation. There are few schools and the ones there are often lack curriculum diversity and facilities (gymnasiums, pools, computer labs, multi-media centers, libraries). In rural areas there are high rates of school dropouts, youth unemployment, and delinquency. (These problems are not confined to the city.) In addition, rural youth often have low educational and occupational aspirations; consequently, they aren't prepared to deal with today's world where even agriculture is scientific.

Community life is often different in small towns where people take the time to get to know one another and become involved in each other's lives. Some migrants move to rural areas to find this community unity. They want to escape the isolation of city life. In reality, in many rural settings, there is great distance between houses. People who move to these areas trade psychological isolation for actual physical isolation. Besides, we've all heard of city tenement dwellers who have banded together in a real community spirit. This will happen in any environment where people take the time to get involved with each other.

THE READER'S TURN:

1. Where is the contrast between ideal and reality first spelled out? How does it help organize the rest of the paper?

2. For many readers, weighing the pros and cons of city versus country is an old familiar topic. How does this paper bring it to life? Does the writer succeed in getting you involved in the topic? Why or why not?

3. Some of this paper moves on a very general level. Overall, what is the balance between generalizations and specific examples?

4. This writer has the knack of using deliberate repetition and parallel structure to drive home a point. Discuss the examples in the second and third paragraphs.

5. Prepare a comparison and contrast of this paper and "The Song and the Dance" in Unit 2 (Observation).

Wolves Mate for Life—Do You?

It is believed that the wolf mates for life. Spring is the breeding season. Six to seven in a litter is usual, but there may be as many as fourteen. The pups are born with big blue eyes, which soon fade in color. The family remains together while the pups are young, even when the mother breeds in successive years, and all members help take care of the family.

This could be compared to the traditional marriages of earlier times--married for life with six to fourteen children, and the family was a unit--unlike some of today's modern marriages where divorce dismantles half of them. What are the differences between the old traditional marriage and the new modern one that is so prominent in today's society? Where do these differences lie? I believe the substantial differences lie in the three general areas of work, family, and education, each stemming from changes in economics, values, or morality, (or the lack of it, depending upon your viewpoint).

My grandpa and grandma lived in the little town of Yuba City and carried on a very traditional marriage. My grandfather did all of the out-of-house work while Grandma preoccupied herself with the domestic duties such as cleaning, cooking, and taking care of the children. My grandfather was a farmer and grew fruit and nut trees. He "brought home the bacon," while Grandma did the frying. This was very common in the traditional marriage for the husband to work and the wife to stay at home, but this isn't too often seen in today's society anymore.

Now we see the modern marriage as the only way to go. Because of the high cost of living both partners must work to support themselves. No longer can the husband deal with the outside job while his wife deals with the household. When I was younger my parents operated on a traditional-style marriage, but when I became a freshman in college, my mother went to work as an accountant. Our family could no longer live on what my father brought home, so my mother's joining the labor force was the only answer.

Family life in the traditional marriage is quite different from that in the modern marriage. My grandparents had three children--two boys, and one girl. Having three or more children was not uncommon, but now in a modern marriage the third is usually "a mistake." My grandparents considered the family to be a very important institution and thus had many family activities together that brought closeness and harmony to the family. They often went camping at a cabin in Mt. Lassen, fed the ducks Wonder Bread at Ellis Lake, and played at the Sutter County park which had four swings, a set of monkey bars, a slide, and a merry-go-round. Vacations were also family-oriented. They would pack the car and drive to Oklahoma to visit family out there, singing "She'll be comin' round the mountain" as they traveled.

In the modern marriage, people often forget the importance of the family. Often there isn't even a whole family present. Half of today's marriages end in divorce, thus leaving a single parent somewhere with children to take care of, and that parent working to support the children usually has little or no time for family activities. Even when both parents are present, often work schedules conflict, and differing individual wants and needs come into play. Dad's been working all week and wants to watch baseball and relax on Saturday, Mom has to work 10 to 6:30, the older child has a book report due on Monday, but the little six-year-old wants to feed the ducks the stale bread with the family. It just doesn't work as well as it used to. Families are lucky if they get a one-week vacation together at Big Basin to camp in an overcrowded tent and fight off savage ants and blood-sucking mosquitoes, eat overripe fruit, and use outhouses that reek and have doors that never quite latch.

Education is something that the whole family participates in a traditional marriage. Not only do the children learn at school, but they are also taught important things at home. My grandma taught her daughter to cook, embroider, can fruits and vegetables, iron, and churn butter. She taught all her kids manners and how to behave. My grandpa taught all his children how to grade fruit--know what is acceptable for market--drive the vehicles, milk the cows, even ride a bike, swim and dive, hunt, and fish. He also taught his sons how to work on mechanical vehicles, prune trees, irrigate, and breed the livestock. He also took time to help his children learn the value of money, by helping them open up a savings account. Other relatives taught the children also. An aunt taught the girl to crochet and her great-grandmother taught her to sew and quilt. The boys' great-grandfather taught them to carve things out of wood.

Things are quite different in the modern marriages we see today. The parents have little time for teaching in the home because of their work responsibilities. Education occurs at school and through peers and other sources, and children learn more on their own without the family than ever before. They attend driving school to learn how to drive, and the local Parks and Recreation Department takes care of the swim lessons. Relatives aren't usually involved as much as in a traditional marriage either. As Ms. magazine says, "Grandma is 61. She looks 45, is divorced, has a job selling real estate, and spends her weekends with a retired banker whose wife died three years ago."

Why have marriages changed? Why aren't families the self-sufficient, close, "all for one and one for all" units they used to be? I believe the change stems from economics. Society hardly allows that type of lifestyle anymore. Values have changed also, along with changes in morality. I don't believe people put as high a priority on marriage and family as they used to. Maybe divorce, suicide, mental and emotional breakdowns, child abuse, incest, adultery, and all the other things that society abhors but has such an abundance of would decrease if people valued marriage and family more, and looked back to some of the traditional marriage ways, and even took after the wolf and mated for life, as it used to be.

THE READER'S TURN:

1. This writer looks at a familiar topic from a fresh perspective. How and with what effect? Are there any striking details or unusual touches in this paper that you are likely to remember?

2. Chart the point-by-point comparison developed in this paper. What are the major points? How well are they supported or followed up?

3. Do the examples in this paper seem representative or one-sided? Does the writer rely exclusively on personal observation?

4. What kind of reader would make an ideal audience for this paper? Do you yourself make a good audience for it? Did it make you reconsider or change your thinking?

5. Compare and contrast two different styles of family life or home life that you have observed or experienced.

And in This Corner!

Can you imagine the President of the United States in attendance at a roller derby game? Probably not, as this would seem as plausible as imagining a member of the local plumbing union spending his vacation money traveling back to Australia to watch the United States win back the coveted America's Cup in yachting competition. Nowhere in America are there more clear-cut boundaries drawn between the upper, middle, and lower-class social levels than those seen in the vast differences between the sporting events members of each class attend. The distinctions between these groups meet the eye (or rather jump out at the eye) in three areas: the kinds of cars the spectators drive to the competitions, the types of clothes the various fans wear, and the commercials shown during the television broadcast of the events.

The traditional upper-class sports include tennis, yachting, golfing and polo. If we were to attend a tennis match at Forest Hills in New York, we would find a subdued and dignified crowd, the majority of them arriving in some type of Mercedes-Benz, Volvo, Saab, Porsche, BMW, or private limousine. The spectators are attired in expensive avant-garde designer labels such as Calvin Klein, Perry Ellis, or Yves St. Laurent, with the majority of the designs consisting of cool and casual white shirts with pastel-colored detailing, tucked into roomy cotton slacks. Feet are usually dressed in either hand-made Italian or Sperry Topsider shoes. The mood at the match is quiet unless, of course, a player like John McEnroe swears at a referee over a bad line call, whereupon a murmur quickly passes through the crowd. Once calm is restored, the spectators resume sipping their Perrier mineral water through straws. For those unfortunate fans unable to attend in person, mostly because of the need to be in another city to close a business deal, a big screen television will provide the action. These tennis fans will be bombarded by commercials for Volvo sedans, IBM and Apple computers, and E.F. Hutton stock offerings, to name but a few.

Middle-class sports include more traditional American pastimes such as football, baseball, and basketball. A visit to the Candlestick Park parking lot prior to a Forty-Niners game produces a scene in which families arrive in Dodge, Ford, and Chevrolet station wagons and vans. The younger fans arrive in Chevy Camaros, Pontiac Trans-Ams, Honda Accords, or any of a myriad of Datsun and Toyota coupes. There is a wider variety of dress in the middle-class crowd as the group consists of personalities that make up the nucleus of the social melting pot of America. The majority, however, are neatly dressed in any number of mass-produced shirts and blouses purchased from Sears, Mervyn's, or J.C. Penney. The pants range from polyester blends that stretch over the older folks' waists to the popular Levis Button-fly 501 jean of the younger crowd. These casual clothes allow the crowd to become somewhat more vocal and rowdy than their counterparts at a tennis match, perhaps because it is easier to wash hot-dog mustard off a pair of Levis than to have a pair of $200 Calvin Klein slacks dry cleaned. At home, the average television viewer is subjected to a barrage of commercials which publicize the latest results in the burger war between McDonald's, Burger King, Wendy's, and Jack-in-the-Box restaurants; the service guaranteed at Midas Muffler shops; and the promises which Lee Iacocca makes assuring the public that Chrysler quality is leading the way in the assault on hostile foreign imports. Of course, one can't overlook the light beer commercials featuring Rodney Dangerfield.

Lower-class sports are in a category all their own. They include All-Star Wrestling, an activity where burly men dressed in skin-tight shorts fake trying to kill each other on a stage resembling a boxing ring, and the classic thriller called roller derby, which is a twisted version of All-Star Wrestling on wheels. The lower-class crowd in attendance usually arrives in an assortment of cars, most of which are gas-guzzling dinosaurs the middle class abandoned as uneconomical after the oil crisis of the early seventies. If the spectators didn't arrive in a car, they either walked or took the bus. Their clothes consist of fashions which went out of style five years ago--clothes which, if new, were purchased during a blue light special at a discount store or at the local flea market. Some of the fans are more up-to-date, however, sporting tee shirts printed with bold letters proclaiming "How Do I Spell Relief? B-E-E-R!" These crowds are usually quite loud and boisterous, largely due to the inordinate amount of alcohol they have consumed. The activities themselves are not usually broadcast on the major television networks, a sign that no advertiser wants to waste his budget appealing to a social group that has no money to spend on his product anyway. You can, however, occasionally catch an episode of the event either immediately following the Saturday morning cartoons or on late night television. If so, you will be treated to commercials pushing products like Black Flag Roach Spray and Elvis Presley's Greatest Hits albums. Special commercials also invite select viewers to enroll in an automotive institute where they will learn how to make big bucks as diesel mechanics.

The question is yet unanswered whether it is the sport itself that draws a particular type of fan or whether the type of fan surrounds a sport with the aura of a particular social class. Which is the chicken, and which is the egg?

THE READER'S TURN:

1. This writer has a sharp eye for characteristic, revealing detail. Point out some striking examples.

2. Do you relate to this author's sense of humor? Why or why not?

3. Sum up what this author's classification of kinds of sports implies about the values, styles, and manners of the three social classes.

4. Find another area (education, religion, fashion) where you think the traditional classification of upper-class, middle-class, and lower-class still applies. Fill in examples or details to help show the validity or relevance of the three categories.

5. Can you think of an area where the traditional scheme of three social classes is no longer relevant or has broken down? What system of classification would you put in its place?

"Bang! Zap! and Pow!": Punk in Retrospect

What exactly is a punk? Smirking caricatures (decked out with multi-colored mohawks and dirty jeans, cheeks and ears pierced with safety pins) come to mind. The punk revolution that began in the music industry has for all intents and purposes been dead for half a decade now. However, the external images persist. They permeate our television and movies. How many T.V. and movie villains have had spiked hair or earrings? When we think of punks, we think of mindless rebellion, of youthful anarchy without direction. Like <u>yippie</u>, <u>hippie</u>, <u>beatnik</u>, or <u>yuppie</u>, the term <u>punk</u> was a convenient way of tagging a pop phenomenon in our culture. We use these images without understanding where they came from or what they originally represented.

By the mid-seventies rock and roll had fallen into a rut of bloated excess. Arena rock, bands performing in huge open-air stadiums, was the rule of the day. Bands were more akin to corporations. The music had become self-indulgent and unwieldy. The music scene was gutted with egotism. Punk came along and thumbed its nose at this establishment. Musically, punk through all of its various guises was undeniably simple. It consisted mainly of three-chord progressions slugged out in jackhammer style on an electric guitar. Lyrically, it was a free-for-all of shouting in a vaguely melodic way. Each song was designed as a KO punch to the intellectual and aesthetic palate. It was simplistic, shocking, and raw. A typical punk show was marked by slam dancing and stage diving, something like <u>Big Time Wrestling</u> speeded up and set to music.

In 1976 a group from New York called "The Ramones" toured England. The first group to break out from the tiny NY punk scene, the Ramones tore across England igniting the imaginations of the young people there. Many latched onto this new trend immediately and made it their own. The punk movement exploded in the United Kingdom. It spread through all areas of the pop culture, into fashion as well as music. So when Johnny Rotten (John Lydon) of the Sex Pistols sang in his pinched holler, "I am an anarchist!" or Joe Strummer of the Clash howled "I'm bored with the USA" to the pained chords of their songs, it signaled rebellion against the established music scene.

Anarchy in the form of the punk revolution stirred the stagnant pool pop music had sunk into. But more so, the English scene reflected the particular plight of European youth in general and British youth specifically. More than half of the youth in England were on government welfare. Music was more than a mode of expression then; it was a chance for economic freedom, a chance to escape the minimal existence the dole allowed. But in England's strenuously competitive music scene, each new band had to be more outrageous, more offensive to attract attention. And within two years the movement through burnout and, particularly in London bands, drugs, stalled and fractured. Many of the pioneers, those who survived the excesses of their stardom, veered into other musical endeavors.

In the early eighties, the punk movement returned to the United States with a vengeance. While many elements of the British scene found themselves in the more commercial "new wave" bands that had emerged from the wreck of the early punk movement, the American punks pursued their art with the fervor of zealous purists. This movement centralized mostly in California and Los Angeles in particular. Bands with names like "X," "Fear," "The Circle Jerks," and "The Dead Kennedys" dealt with uniquely American themes. Many British bands had lashed out against the traditional aristocracy; the Americans rejected the values of their country's affluent middle class represented by the endless housing tracts of suburbia. The Brits were obsessed with pop stardom while the Yanks fervently rejected it. In fashion they were less gaudy than their English counterparts, and while some British bands such as the Clash aligned themselves with left-wing socialists, the Americans stayed way from mainstream politics. They found middle-class living both morally and artistically stifling. They saw commercial America as represented by its television, movies, fashion, and pop music, as a factory churning out an endless array of clones instead of encouraging free thinking and acting youth. Typically, they punctuated their ideas with gratuitous violence on stage. But their main intent was to shake up, not destroy.

Punk rock was never a very complex art form, and so by around 1982 it was fished out of original ideas. The punks had run out of ways to vent their rage. It all began to sound the same. Many such as Phil Alven of the Blasters and X turned to the roots movement, exploring the folk roots of American music. Ironically, others entered into the commercial mainstream they had so vehemently proselytized against. However, there were many youths who were still in elementary school when the Sex Pistols thrashed about in 1977. They were unwilling to let punk lie in its grave. And so "hardcore" was born. The tag applies to a great many bands that popped up in the aftermath around the country. This is the greatest in-joke that many of these hardcore bands don't understand. By simply rehashing the same stale themes of rebellion and self-expression through expletives and stage violence, the hardcore bands are simply conforming. Instead of changing the music, they perpetuate and freeze what has already been done, committing the same crimes that so enraged the founders. Originality has left the movement, and as a viable force in the music world it has faded.

Punk, which never made it as a long-term alternative, instead was an effective antidote to the lethargic music of the mid- and late-seventies. The revolution was an internal one, a definite reaction to what was happening at the time in the industry. It's foolish to endow punk with too lofty motives, but it was more than mindless violence. It was focused rage at systems that had become so rigid that creativity had been frozen out. It was a stripped-down approach to pop music. But now, as memories in our information overloaded society are proving ever shorter, we have lost a picture of what it was. Only the spitting, swearing caricature, the hardcore caricature, remains.

THE READER'S TURN:

1. Does the reader have to be an insider or fan to appreciate this paper? Does it have something to offer the uninitiated outsider?
2. What are the major kinds or stages of punk sketched out by this writer? According to this paper, what were its original motives or inspiration? What went wrong?
3. Do you think this writer takes the social or political implications of pop music too seriously?
4. Introduce the uninitiated reader to the characteristic lingo or shoptalk of a particular school of artists or musicians.

5. Look at some area that you know well as a fan or insider—cars, popular music, classical music, theater, crafts. Set up a system of classification that allows you to put your own tastes or preferences in context. Identify and illustrate major kinds or stages.

WRITING TOPICS 3

Readers appreciate writers who help them make sense of what is difficult or confusing. There is often a ready-made audience for writers who know how to make information accessible, how to help us make something work, or how to guide us in making tricky choices. Practice laying out material in such a way that your readers will say: "At first I was confused, but now I see!"

1. How It Works: Americans increasingly suffer from the black-box mentality. We push a button to activate a gadget or resource, but we no longer understand what is inside the "black box" to make it work. Help your readers overcome the black-box mentality. Explain the inner workings of a microwave oven, a laser printer, a compact disk player, or similar device. Or explain the miracle of the microchip, the workings of a kidney machine, the technology of a high-performance engine.

2. Guidelines: Advice columns guide readers through changing patterns of love and courtship. Chart for your readers the new etiquette for dating, getting married, or getting divorced. (Is love at first sight obsolete? Should women ask men out for dates? Who should pay? Should parents have a say about a child's marriage? What are sufficient reasons for getting a divorce?)

3. Lifestyles: Lifestyles different from our own at times seem bizarre until someone explains to us the background and mentality of the people who practice them. Compare and contrast two lifestyles to help readers understand a way that might be different from their own. For instance, compare and contrast in detail single and married, motorist and cyclist, junk-food addict and health food fanatic, artist and yuppie, the studious type and the athletic type, party animals and loners, rich and poor.

4. Types: Everyone hates to be stereotyped. But teachers, counselors, coaches, or employers recognize certain types nevertheless. Set up a scheme of classification that would help your readers recognize and deal with several major types—of students, of athletes, of employees, of dating partners, of customers, or the like.

5. Upgrades: Provide help for readers who want to upgrade their surroundings, their performance, or their lives. For instance, demonstrate for them the difference between tacky and classy, or between perennial worker and management potential, or between klutzy and suave.

4
The Active Reader: Writing from Sources

Good writers are usually alert and active readers. Their reading is for them a constantly replenished source of material. From their reading, they get new ideas, expert opinions to quote, important evidence to cite, and provocative questions to explore. People who read little often have sparsely furnished minds. As a result, their writing is likely to be short on background information, striking examples, important precedents, and backup from authoritative sources.

The student papers in this group draw on the students' current reading. The writers have not conducted the kind of in-depth investigation that we would expect in a full-fledged research paper. Instead, they have read up on a topic of current interest in order to find expert opinion and up-to-date information. To make good use of their reading, these writers had to

- *select* key facts, important information, quotable quotes
- *integrate* or synthesize material from a variety of sources
- *attribute* the material they used by identifying their sources

The first writer identifies sources informally in the text itself, the way a writer would in a magazine intended for the general reader. The other two writers give full information about sources in a final bibliography, or list of "Works Cited," the way a writer would in a scholarly or professional periodical.

Man with a Mission

American history has often been taught out of textbooks giving an expurgated and generally uplifting version of our country's past. However, in recent years we have frequently heard voices asking us to remember a forgotten page in our history or to revise a biased chapter. On the occasion of the beatification of Father Junipero Serra, descendants of the "mission Indians" asked us to reexamine the relationship between the Spanish missionaries and the native Americans they set out to convert.

The Computer as Teacher

Increasingly, computers do our calculating, record-keeping, data processing, and planning for us. Increasingly, they also help us learn and write. This writer did some background reading to find authoritative opinion on the strengths and weaknesses of the teaching done by computers.

The Artificial Heart

What are the realities behind the media hype that surrounds "medical miracles" or "breakthroughs"? This writer's reading focused on the soul-searching and second thoughts that followed the first experimental uses of the artificial heart.

Man with a Mission

Assimilation, from a sociological viewpoint, is the process whereby a minority or immigrant group gradually adopts the characteristics of another culture. The native American Indians converted to Christianity through Father Junipero's "mission system" illustrate a group that underwent such a process of assimilation. History shows, however, that as these Indians assimilated into the "mission system," they lost their culture, their freedom, and their ethnic dignity.

Living in the Bay Area, we can appreciate the rich Spanish heritage that the figure of Father Junipero Serra vividly symbolizes. El Camino Real, which means the King's Highway, stretches from San Diego to San Francisco and remarkably parallels, at most points, Father Serra's "sacred expedition" of 1769. At the time of his appointment as Father-president of the missions in Alta California, he was 55 years old. He held the post until he died in 1784 at the age of 70. During his lifetime, he built 12 missions, but at what cost to the Indians?

The first stage of assimilation for the Indians began when they involuntarily changed their own religion, an integral part of their culture, to Christianity. For Serra the Indians were heathens; their rites pagan. His "sacred expedition" was to convert them to Christianity. According to an article in the September 26 issue of the Mercury News, written by Joan Connell, its religion and ethics editor, the church's attitude toward the Indians' culture remains unchanged. Andrew Galvin, whose family is descended from Ohlone Indians converted by Serra more than

200 years ago, had been invited by the Vatican to participate in the beatification of Father Junipero Serra by Pope John Paul II. Galvin, a former Franciscan brother, who is now secretary to the Rev. Noel Moholy, chief agent of Serra's campaign for sainthood, wanted to present an heirloom Ohlone basket, filled with acorns, along with the other gifts that were to be presented to the pope at the offertory of the Mass. "But some Vatican official felt the acorns weren't appropriate and insisted Andy bring up a gold chalice instead," Moholy said. "We ended up giving the holy father the basket of acorns, but it was given privately later." Then as Galvin, wearing an Ohlone necklace of beads and bone over his suit coat and tie, carried the gold chalice in one hand and a brace of eagle feathers in the other, a Vatican official tried to snatch the eagle feather from his hand at one point during the procession. But Galvin resisted. When interviewed later, Galvin had this to say: "It was the most moving experience, emotionally." The five feathers in his hand had represented his father and mother, himself, and his brother and sister. "I felt I not only presented myself to the pope but those who are near and dear to me. In the end, I was enraptured. There was a flood of tears and such wonderful joy." This man, apparently, is caught in the middle, torn between assimilation and a compelling need to express his cultural heritage, willing to incur the wrath of his religious superiors; at the same time assimilated well enough to accept the Church's attitude, a feat that seems to reveal a strong faith.

    The second stage of assimilation for the Indians occurred when they lost their freedom to the "mission system." According to Walter Bean, Professor of History at U.C. Berkeley and the author of <u>California: An Interpretative History</u> (1973), the question of whether the Indians in the California missions were exploited and wretched or contented and appreciative will long remain a moot one. The missionaries generated most of the "preponderant testimony" which describes the mission Indians as happy and well adjusted, preferring mission life to their previous freedom, and grateful for close supervision, hard work, colorful rituals, and the salvation of their souls (63). What is missing in this idyllic picture is any mention of their "terrifying" death rate. The California mission registers, for example, recorded more than twice as many deaths as births, mainly because of disease. Bean attributed it to the Indians' lack of immunity but also the improper sanitary conditions that resulted from the Indians being confined within the adobe walls (63).

"Just like the Christian Jesus said, 'Forgive them, Great Spirit, for they know not what they do,' we pray: Forgive them, Great Spirit, for they know not what they do." These words, reported by Ann W. O'Neill, a <u>Mercury News</u> staff writer, and spoken by Anthony Miranda, a Costanoan Indian in the basilica of the Carmel Mission, on the same day that Serra was being beatified in Rome, drew "shocked gasps and stares at what many of the worshippers considered a sacrilege." Responding to a man's voice in the back of the basilica loudly calling out, "Why don't you take your pagan rites and get out of this church?" the group of twenty Indians carrying ceremonial rattles, feathers, and abalone shells filled with burning sage retreated to the church cemetery. They assembled at the foot of a crude wooden cross that marks the graves of "2,364 Christian Indians and 14 Spaniards," buried there between 1771 and 1833.

The third stage of assimilation for the Indians resulted in their loss of ethnic dignity. I am using the term <u>ethnic</u> as it pertains "to a social group within a cultural and social system that claims or is accorded special status on the basis of complex, often variable traits including religious, linguistic, ancestral, or physical characteristics" (<u>The American Heritage Dictionary</u>). For the Indians this "special status" meant prejudicial stereotyping and brutal treatment. According to the Comte de La Perouse, a French nobleman who visited Monterey in 1782 as part of a global voyage of scientific investigation, the Indian under the mission system was "too much a child, too much a slave, too little a man," and in the Spaniards' resort to stocks, irons, and the lash, and the use of soldiers to hunt down those who tried to escape, there was a distressing resemblance to the slave plantations he had seen in Santo Domingo (51). How the Indians were stereotyped is illustrated for us in a letter boosting California, written by Governor Diego de Borica (1794-1800), a jovial Basque. It makes a significant reference to the Spanish way of distinguishing the two main groups of colonial population in Monterey: There was "good bread, excellent meat, tolerable fish, and good humor which is worth all the rest. Plenty to eat, but the most astounding is the general fecundity, both of rationals and irrationals." According to Bean, the <u>gente de razon</u>, the people of reason, included all who were not full-blooded Indians (54). He points out, moreover, that the padres always applied the term "neophytes," or apprentices in Christianity, even to Indians who had been born in the missions and spent their entire lives there. "The belief that any group of human adults could be happy under a system that treated them as if they were hopelessly retarded children was a very questionable one" (63).

What is the difference between the Christian God and the Castanoan Indian's "Great Spirit," or the Church's ceremonial robes and rites of incense and the Castanoans' ceremonial robes and incense? Why must one race be a beast of burden for another, and what is it that makes one race superior? In the end, it is our ignorance that remains the one constant continuum in the history of mankind.

THE READER'S TURN:

1. The opening paragraph raises the central issue of assimilation. How does it call the conventional definition of assimilation into question?

2. What striking details early in the paper help dramatize the traditional attitude of the church toward the Native Americans?

3. Much modern history is "revisionist" history—asking us to revise or reconsider long accepted views. How does this paper affect or change your assumptions about the missionary effort and mission life? Which of the author's key terms or key challenges becomes most meaningful to you?

4. What is the mix of sources that this paper draws on? What are some striking or effective uses of direct quotation?

5. To follow up, investigate the role of the missionary effort or the role of the church in colonizing other parts of the New World—for instance, New England, Mexico, the Southwest. What sources can you find? Do they show a particular bias? Do they point toward a current consensus?

The Computer as Teacher

A few years ago I enrolled in a CAI (computer assisted instruction) program at City College. I had a major problem with spelling words, so I decided to seek help at the college's Learning Assistance Center. The center had computer programs that took the student, step by step, through exercises like video games. First, the computer showed me the correct spelling of a difficult and commonly misspelled word. Next, it would show me what context the word was used in. Finally, the computer gave me several sentences to spell the word in. After a particular program was finished, the computer would calculate my score in percentages. Being like a game, it was a fun way to learn. Although I had fun with the machine, I did not interact in any way with anybody in the center while I was there. There are many advantages and disadvantages in using computers as teachers. In one sense computers are more efficient than human teachers, but human teachers are more sensitive to human values.

Computers as teachers can be programmed for an extremely wide range of ability levels. For instance, if a student were doing a math problem that required a formula but couldn't get the right answer because he didn't have the right formula, the computer would drop down to the student's abilities to accommodate him. Conversely, the computer could raise up a level if the need came up. In the traditional classroom setting, placement tests help to avoid these ability differences, but the teacher cannot meet every student's level of competency as well as a computer can. In a book called <u>The Computer in the School: Tutor, Tool, and Tutee</u>, R. Taylor writes that "human instruction rarely aims to accommodate individual differences because the normal classroom situation prohibits such accommodation" (3). In other words the teacher cannot speak to an individual student's needs as computers can. Computers can adjust for individual discrepancies in IQ (102). Since this is not a problem for the computer, the computer as teacher will be more efficient.

With the exactness of hand calculators, computers could chart a student's progress much more efficiently than humans. As Taylor shows, "diagnosis and evaluation" of students' progress could be exactly charted with exercise and test scores (103). Also, with this efficiency there would be no misunderstandings that sometimes occur between student and teacher.

Working with a computer is much different than with human teachers. Conflicting student and teacher roles are displaced when the computer as teacher comes into play (122). Traditionally, when a student receives a negative response for an incorrect answer, he or she can take it personally or resent the teacher, but with the computer the student does not take it personally because it's a machine. As a result the student becomes much more intellectually active (122).

This heightened intellectual activity furthermore seems to give rise to intense communication among peers about computer-related topics. In an article from Psychology Today entitled "Computers and Kids: The Good News," Gilbert Levin, a professor of psychiatry at the Albert Einstein College of Medicine in New York, writes that cooperation among children who use computers is very high, and the hope is that this can be transferred to the "broader context of interpersonal relationships" (51).

Although there are some real advantages for the use of computers as teachers, there are many real disadvantages also. The first major disadvantage is that computers to a certain extent think for students. With the advent of calculators, all students have to do is press a few buttons to achieve correct answers. With computers this concept can be magnified a hundred times over because computers are a kind of super-calculator. Children in the future may not be taught to do arithmetic mentally and quickly (15). Instead students might be taught to press the correct buttons. Mark R. Lepper in his article, "Microcomputers in Education," raises an important question: "Will the 3Rs, in short, be replaced by the 4Cs--comprehension, composition, calculation, and computing?" (15). Only time will tell what people will think is more important.

Writing in Contemporary Education, Michael J. Carbone ("Computers in Education: A Cautious View") cites another possible negative effect: the "Big Brother Syndrome." Will teachers be constantly watched for declining performance? Computers as teachers calculate everything so well that administrators could exercise closer supervision even when they are not around (209). Another way of stating this is that supervisors and managers could "increase surveillance without depending on face to face supervision" (210).

The biggest possible threat is the total displacement of the teacher. Computers would be able to run every aspect of the educational show save for programming themselves. The human teacher would become at best merely a technician or machine operator. Moreover, the teachers' alienation by computers would result in deskilling and degrading (210).

Students too can experience a kind of alienation. Students who spend a great deal of time working with computers as teachers would of course have less time for other activities. These persons would have less time for things like reading, sports, social activities, or informal play. This immersion could "prove that each man is an island unto himself" (210). Students would interact more with computers than with professionals. To quote Lepper again: "There is a potential for children becoming introverted social isolates, eight-year old 'hackers' and video game addicts" (15). If not completely introverted, students nevertheless could have less communication with teachers, administrators, and other students.

The computer as teacher can have both positive and negative effects. It can be programmed to fit many IQs, chart progress efficiently, and heighten intellectual activity. Conversely, the computer can take away human values. It can make people less likely to use their own emotional and logical inner workings. The computer can take away one's own ability to work problems mentally, institute "Big Brother" supervision on performances, and reduce human contact. My own opinion is that we must pay very close attention to what the computer can and cannot do, or else our children might get an education with the kinds of values that promote machines only.

Works Cited

Broudy, Harry S. "Teaching Machines: Threats and Promises." <u>The Education Digest</u> 28 (Nov. 1962): 100-103.

Carbone, Michael J. "Computers in Education: A Cautious View." <u>Contemporary Education</u> (Summer 1985): 209-210.

Dalton, David W., Michael J. Hannafin. "The Role of Computer-Assisted Instruction in Affecting Learner Self-

Esteem." <u>Education Technology</u> (Dec. 1984): 43.

Lepper, Mark R. "Microcomputers in Education: Motivation and Social Issues." <u>American Psychology</u> (Jan. 1985): 15-16.

Levin, Gilbert. "Computers and Kids: The Good News." <u>Psychology Today</u> (Aug. 1985): 51.

Taylor, Robert P. <u>The Computer in the School: Tutor, Tool and Tutee</u>. New York: Teacher's College Press, 1980.

THE READER'S TURN:

1. How does this paper dramatize the issue? Where and how does it lead up to its central thesis?

2. According to this writer, what are the advantages of computerized instruction? How does he show and document them?

3. What are the disadvantages? How does the writer show and document them?

4. How well does this paper balance the pro and con? Does it favor one side or the other? How would *you* balance the pro and con?

5. To update this writer's treatment of the subject, find several more recent sources. Do they confirm or do they make you modify this writer's findings?

The Artificial Heart

Could you imagine walking into a small room in an intensive care unit to visit someone you have known and loved over the years? He or she is, for the most part, bedridden. His or her life is totally dependent on being connected and confined to a 323-pound pneumatic system. This machine keeps your loved one's artificial heart functioning.

Just several weeks after surgery when things were beginning to look brighter, your loved one begins to have multiple episodes of seizures in which he/she becomes unconscious. At this time, the surgeon tells you that there is cerebral hemorrhage and evidence of a stroke. Your loved one now is partially paralyzed and his/her speech is badly slurred. A speech therapist visits daily helping this patient to communicate, but often within minutes this patient forgets everything said previously. These new neurological problems are likely to last as long as your loved one's artificial heart keeps working. One such patient previously lasted 620 days. Most of his days were spent with loss of memory, severe depression, and helplessness. You continue to visit and be supportive in what has turned into a nightmarish situation for you and your loved one. At this point, you cannot help but question this existence. What at first felt like a medical miracle has turned into a grim, degrading experience for the person you love.

As of 1986, all artificial heart recipients had suffered from such complications along with pneumonia and kidney failure. Dr. John Watson, Chief of the Devices and Technology Branch of the National Heart, Lung and Blood Institute states, "It certainly has been a sobering experience" (Lord and Carey 8). Most experts believe that the use of permanent artificial hearts will be rare unless designers can develop a full implantable model with increased safeguards against strokes. Both medical and scientific professionals have vigorously debated the issues regarding this at first seemingly irresistible medical technology. Starting in 1964, the National Heart, Lung and Blood Institute provided 180 million dollars for the development of the artificial heart and related devices.

These are some of the important issues and questions raised by both biochemical scientists and heart surgeons: Is it ethical to continue research with this mechanical heart using human experimentation? Could the enormous cost with federal funding involved be better spent in preventive health care education? Is it ethical to involve heroic interventions to extend people's lives without any guarantee as to the quality of life they will experience after the implantation of this mechanical device? Is there a place at all for the artificial heart? Will it be a valuable new device that could save people's lives or will it only prolong dying and be an enormous financial drain on medical resources?

Some of these questions were debated in 1986 by artificial heart inventor Robert Jarvik of Symbion, Inc. in Salt Lake City, and scientist Daniel Callahan of the Hastings Center, a biomedical-ethics research institute in

Hastings-on-Hudson, New York. Jarvik pointed out the experience of the Swedish recipient of the artificial heart whose life was extended seven-and-a-half months with this device. Jarvik was very impressed with the recipient's ability to climb five flights of stairs during this time. However, the recipient died of cerebral bleeding associated with the mechanical heart implantation. The recipient's surgeon, Dr. Semb, stated, "He might as well have died to begin with" ("Artificial Heart" 122). Callahan continued to argue that "we're not going to create healthy people with long life expectancies . . . we're going to create people who are going to be chronically ill" ("Artificial Heart" 122). He further felt that the use of the artificial heart was not solely for the recipient to debate but for society as a whole. Callahan gave the estimated figures by the National Heart, Lung and Blood Institute that there exist 17,000 to 35,000 potential recipients each year at a cost of $150,000 per implant, possibly adding between 2.5 billion to 5 billion to the United States' medical bill. He believes that such money could be better spent on preventive health education to fight heart disease. On the other hand, Jarvik remained convinced that the artificial heart might allow people to remain productive in society and noted that 3 billion is spent on video games each year.

An earlier meeting of leading transplant surgeons sponsored by the Foundation for American Communications had been held in Washington D.C. October 24th and 25th, 1985. At this meeting, it was made clear that even these transplant surgeons were unable to agree on where to go next with the artificial heart device. Jack Copeland, a heart surgeon from Tucson who pioneered the use of the mechanical heart as a temporary bridge until a permanent heart is available, said that referrals had diminished since the complications involved with the artificial heart transplant had become so evident. Recipients are informed and concerned about bleeding, strokes, and kidney failure associated with the implant.

On the other hand, O.H. Frazier, Director of the Cardiac and Pulmonary Transplant Program at the Texas Heart Institute in Houston, argued that such complications using the artificial heart needed to be put in better perspective. "The amazing thing to me is how well it's done. We had more problems with it in animals than we do in people and after all you have to remember that these are dying patients" (Kolata 786). Frazier thought that 100 artificial heart implantations would have to be performed before a really accurate conclusion could be drawn about the true potential of the mechanical heart.

The position voiced by Dr. Copeland is that "the most logical course of action is to use the artificial heart only as a temporary device since the laboratory results indicate that it always fails" (Wallis 8). The artificial heart has a potential for a bridge until a donor heart is found and made available for transplant. However, others have argued that using the artificial heart as a temporary device is not practical because there only so many available hearts. Keeping numbers of people on mechanical hearts would not help solve the already existing problem of a limited human heart supply.

Jarvik has remained the leading voice claiming that permanent artificial heart implantation will make good sense. He has speculated that the younger 20 and 30-year-old heart attack patients will be given priority for heart transplantations. And with hearts unavailable, older patients might accept the mechanical device as an alternative to death. Jarvik has projected the possibility of prolonging the life of an individual for twenty years. He has said, "My company is working on a battery-powered device worn in a vest." According to him, "a completely internal power source would have to be nuclear, and such a device is unlikely to be accepted by the public or the medical community" ("Artificial Heart" 122).

Generally I feel there will always be a percentage of our society who will take any risks to obtain a bit of immortality. I personally would not give my mortality away to live a few additional months only to experience a growing helplessness and loss of personal integrity. I would rather be dead than to stare blankly during the majority of my waking hours. Not to be in control of my body functions and to be unable to communicate would be worse than death. Also I would not like to see someone I love go through the agony that recipients of the artificial heart experience. When a highly educated scientist considers putting internal nuclear devices inside of human beings, I cannot help but think that technology is diminishing our respect for life. Barton J. Bernstein, a historian at Stanford University, reflects on technological decision making as a whole and asks, "Why is it that technological 'fixes' or 'solutions' seem more attractive than preventive activities?" He suggests "it is because prevention does not involve a dramatic hero or event" ("Heart Attack" 81).

Works Cited

"Artificial Heart: The Debate Goes On." *Science News* 129 (22 Feb. 1986): 122.

Brazell, Robert. "Hearts of Gold." *New Republic* 92 (18 Feb. 1985): 17-21.

Carey, Joseph. "Artificial Hearts: Imaginative and Costly." *U.S. News and World Report* (10 Dec. 1984): 62.

"Heart Attack." *Scientific American* 255 (Dec. 1986): 81.

Kolata, Gina. "Surgeons Disagree on the Artificial Heart." *Science* 230 (Nov. 1985): 786-87.

Lord, Lewis J. and Joseph Carey. "Man-Made Hearts: A Grim Prognosis." *U.S. News and World Report* 18 (Aug. 1986): 8.

Wallis, Claudia. "Bridging the Gap: A New Role for Artificial Hearts." *Time* 11 (Nov. 1985): 78.

THE READER'S TURN:

1. How does this writer dramatize her topic? Where does she first strike the keynote? Where or how does she sound it again?

2. What, according to this writer, are the key issues? How does she treat or cover them in this paper?

3. Do you feel you are given enough factual information in this paper? What are some of the more important facts and figures provided by the writer?

4. What authorities does the writer cite or invoke in her paper? Does she give both sides a fair hearing?

5. What was the original reception, or what is the current thinking, in relation to other great "steps forward" in medical technology—for example, the kidney machine, the pacemaker? What sources can you identify? Is there any consensus or unanimity among the experts?

WRITING TOPICS 4

1. Buzzwords: For many newspaper readers, the buzzwords of current political debate remain fuzzy and second-hand. Find an article that does an exceptional job of bringing one of these to life for the uninitiated reader. Choose a topic like the "feminization of poverty, "welfare dependency," "pro-choice," "bilingual education," "English as official language," or "French as the official language of Quebec." Write a paper in which you share what you have learned with the uninitiated reader. Quote, paraphrase, explain; if you can, add examples and illustrations of your own.

2. Taking Issue: Find an article that as a whole makes a strong statement on an issue you care about. Choose one sentence that for you best sums up the author's position. Or sum up the author's position in a sentence of your own. Start your paper with that sentence. Then use the rest of your paper to explain and support the author's stand or take issue with it.

3. Listening to Both Sides: Choose an issue on which you have been or still are undecided. Find two articles that approach the issue from different or opposing points of view. Show the difference in the positions of the two authors. Choose a topic like work fare for welfare recipients, mandatory registration of people who have Aids, rent control in your college town, mandatory jail for drunk drivers, banning *Playboy*.

4. Devil's Advocate: When we strongly disagree with others, we can learn a great deal by not brushing off opposing arguments but listening carefully instead. On a current issue, find one or more sources that argue in favor of a position different from your own. Write a paper in which you show that you fully understand the arguments of the other side.

5. Update: Read up on the best current thinking on an issue about which experts have recently changed their minds. For instance, synthesize some of the current thinking about cholesterol, electroshock treatments, bypass surgery, or long-range effects of smoking marijuana.

5
Definition: Weighty Words

Disillusioned voters often feel that what they hear from candidates is just words, words, words. We soon become suspicious of people who use big words too glibly. Writers who want to be taken seriously need to convince the reader that to them words are not just words. They know how to give concrete substance to words that might sound fuzzy or insincere. They know how to anticipate the question of the reader who asks: "What exactly do you mean?"

Definition maps out the territory covered by important words. When we write to define, we may be writing to justify a term that carries an important judgment or charge, to champion a concept that has become the rallying cry for a cause, or to clarify a term that has been batted back and forth in current controversy. What was the agenda for the writers of the following definition papers?

Macho

Macho is the kind of term that sums up but at the same time implies a criticism of a type of person or a lifestyle. This writer spells out the implied criticism, supplying many provocative examples.

Doublespeak

Doublespeak is a pointed, blunt term that has become an effective indictment of the abuses it stands for. This writer analyzes its motives and its workings, making us observe it in its natural habitat.

Secular Humanism

This writer takes an emotionally charged and often very damaging term and tries to get at the root of the controversy surrounding it. The paper serves a familiar purpose of definition: to provide less heat and more light.

Fundamentalism

To explain the role of a phenomenon again strongly evident in American life, this writer draws on personal first-hand experience with it and on a study of its historical roots.

Macho

As a teenager, I used the term <u>macho</u> frequently, as everyone did. It was a catchy word used popularly to describe the preferred male of the decade: slim, tan, furry-chested, gold-chained, and resembling John Travolta. Times have changed, and so have my own definitions. As a grown woman, I have come to realize that with the change in hairstyles, fashion, and the move from the discotheque to the boardroom, the macho man merely changes hats with the times. Macho is not a fashion, a car, or a look; it is an attitude, a way of life.

Why some men choose this particular lifestyle I am sure has something to do with their deep, dark childhood and upbringing. It is often passed down from father to son. A man's attitudes toward women and their respective roles seem to be coded in the Y-chromosome and passed on to his boys. Many just do not seem to realize that the "Me Tarzan—you Jane" scene went out with the Mesozoic Era. The macho man never includes a woman in public conversation. If she dares to enter into the circle of speakers, he gives her no chance to speak. If she approves his own opinion, he gloats. If her view is antagonistic to his, he instantly shoots her down, as her thoughts are only to run along the lines of which brand of detergent is the most economical. Men do not know when to let the woman speak her mind, to explain her own intelligently organized answer to the problem at hand.

The most dangerous macho man is the one who tries to appear caring and considerate. This is the mechanic who worries for your safety and insists on doing six-hundred dollars of work on a fan belt. This is the doctor who tells you that the sharp pain in your knee is merely PMS. "Take some Midol and get plenty of rest," he'll say. This is the wimpy electrical engineer who searches for the mythical four-feet, ten-inch tall, quiet, obedient Asian woman for a wife. He primitively believes that they have all been raised to honor and care for the human male.

The macho man lives his life according to a status ladder. Men are at the top, women at the bottom, while dogs and armadillos are somewhere in between. The thirst for power, the lust for conquest are what he is driven by. Where did it all begin? We women can only blame ourselves for letting it go on for so long, or even allowing it to happen in the first place. We have somehow failed to train the young male to diaper the baby, clean the toilet, and attend the wife's business banquet, while she may design a spaceship, end World War Three, or fight a forest fire.

Some men gladly never achieve the macho state. In fact, many new role models for men have come down the media pathways: Jimmy Stewart, Tom Selleck, and Superman, himself. They are all mild-mannered, shy clods, who for some reason are extremely attractive to the female of the species. So, macho man, no need to change your clothes, shave your chest, or stop eating meat; merely give a little time and well-earned respect to the other half of humanity.

THE READER'S TURN:

1. Brainstorm the term *macho*. What associations, memories, images, or ideas does it bring to mind? Then compare the results of your brainstorming with the ideas and images conjured up in this paper. How much overlap is there? What are some of the important differences, and how do you explain them?

2. How would you sum up this writer's definition of *macho* in one sentence? How would you sum it up in one paragraph?

3. In this paper, the key term triggers an outpouring of eloquent personal testimony. Focus on one of the writer's statements or on one part of her paper. Show in some detail why you agree or disagree.

4. Some people tell young women to be more assertive. Others tell them that they are too aggressive or too assertive already. Do you think this writer is too aggressive or too polemical? Do you think she will alienate all of her male readers? part of her female readers? Why or why not?

5. Current talk about relations between the sexes is abuzz with terms that sum up gender stereotypes or sex roles: *wimp, bimbo, casanova, earth mother, tease, Jewish mother*. Define one such term; analyze and illustrate its uses and implications.

Doublespeak

The army was recently awarded a Doublespeak Award for replacing the word <u>kill</u> with the phrase <u>service the target</u>. A patient died because a nurse mistakenly put a wrong fluid in an intravenous feeding tube, and the coroner classified it as a <u>therapeutic misadventure</u>. A teacher's note informed parents that "there will be a modified English course offered for those children who achieve deficiency in English." All of these examples are perversion of the language—doublespeak. Such language appears to be earnest and meaningful, but it's a mixture of sense and nonsense. The language is inflated and involved, often deliberately ambiguous. Mario Pei in his book <u>Doublespeak in America</u> describes doublespeak as "intentional slants, distortions, and outright coinages inspired by a purpose of profit, propaganda, or, at the least, personal or institutional prestige." While the English language ought to be used to convey meaning, doublespeak is a method of obscuring meaning. The essence of communication is that words should mean roughly the same to the receiver as the sender. The essence of doublespeak is to distort words so meaning is obscured for the purpose of impressing and bamboozling the reader or hearer.

Theodore Roosevelt called popular attention to doublespeak terms by calling them "weasel words," saying, "When a weasel sucks an egg the meat is sucked out of the egg; and if you use a weasel word after another, there is nothing left of the other." A weasel word does not have to be attached to another word, however. The term has been extended to cover any word deliberately obscured. In the Pentagon, in business, in law, the arts, sciences, education, sports, any field of human endeavor there are examples of weasel words and doublespeak where terms are twisted out of their original meanings and forced into new shapes by the pseudo-intellectual or the pseudo-expert. For those who don't feel comfortable with ordinary words, modifier nouns are invented to dress up words. <u>Curriculum unit</u> is used for <u>courses</u>, <u>student population</u> for <u>students</u>, and <u>highway systems</u> for <u>highway</u>.

For the pseudo-intellectual the object is to impress; for others doublespeak can be used to cover up or deceive. For example, a "negative cash flow" sounds better that "no cash." The personnel office may have an "outplacement counselor" to help an employee who has been fired get a job somewhere else. <u>Outplacement</u> becomes a polite, subtle term for being forced out of a job.

Modern writers have been fascinated with attempts to manipulate language. George Orwell brought us <u>newspeak</u>, the official language of the totalitarian government in his book <u>1984</u>. Jonathan Green, in his book <u>Newspeak, a Dictionary of Jargon</u>, describes Orwell's newspeak as language "designed to shrink vocabularies, to eliminate subtlety, to destroy nuance and to let loose a verbal holocaust upon the English language." Its intentions were to narrow progressively the range of ideas and independent thought. Green describes it as "mellifluous, calming phrases, designed to allay suspicions, modify facts and divert one's attention from difficulties." Newspeak effectively squashed critical thinking.

Although doublespeak is the opposite of newspeak in method, it has similar overtones of the Orwellian nightmare of mass propaganda used to herd people in a chosen direction. When used by agencies like the Pentagon, doublespeak ceases to be laughable and becomes deadly serious instead. A deadly missile becomes a <u>Peacekeeper</u> and bombing becomes <u>air support</u>. The motive of this propaganda is understatement since the merchandise they are selling is death. Manipulators and pseudo-experts use doublespeak to distort meaning, hide truths, and advance their hidden agenda. They know the power of dishonest language.

THE READER'S TURN:

1. What's wrong with the examples of doublespeak that the writer uses in the introduction to bring the topic into focus? Analyze and annotate the examples.

2. To judge from this paper, several motives combine to generate examples of doublespeak. Sort out and list these motives; explain and illustrate each. (Is there a common denominator?)

3. What is the connection between Orwell's newspeak and today's doublespeak?

4. Scan current newspapers for examples of doublespeak—in government, in education, in law, or in any other field. Help your class organize to sift entries for your own Doublespeak Award.

5. Writers who know the power of words have by the same token often been critical of the possible abuses of language. Investigate, define, and illustrate a term like *propaganda, insinuation, indoctrination,* the *hard sell, hype, spiel, pollyanna, evasion.*

Secular Humanism

"Secular humanism" is a sticky little term that has been cropping up lately on television and in our newspapers. Most recently, the phrase "secular humanism" has appeared in pieces covering court cases dealing with textbook banning. It is important to understand the meaning of "secular humanism" not only to be able to understand the media coverage but also to be able to determine a personal stance on this controversial subject.

According to the New World Dictionary, humanism is a system of thought based on the nature, dignity, an ideals of man; "specifically a modern, non-theistic, rationalist movement that holds that man is capable of self-fulfillment, ethical conduct, etc. . . . without recourse to supernaturalism." New World also defines secular as "relating to worldly things as distinguished from things relating to church and religion; not sacred or religious . . ." Combining these two definitions produces an explanation of secular humanism which might read something like this: A person who is separate from any religious organizations or beliefs in spiritual powers is still able to live a completely moral and happily fulfilled life.

Not all interest groups agree with this definition. Groups with strong religious beliefs do not believe that people who are secular humanists are capable of obtaining sound morals on their own. James Hitchcock, author of What Is Secular Humanism?, defines the term in a much more negative way. He writes ". . . the adjective secular comes from the Latin saeculum which means time or age. To call someone secular means that he is completely time-bound, totally a child of his age . . . [his] moral standards, for example, tend to be merely those commonly accepted by the society in which he lives, and he believes everything changes, so that there are no enduring or permanent values." For Hitchcock and many other people with strong religious beliefs, the morals that a humanist has are faulty because they are determined by the surroundings, not by God. The controversy begins here. When parents with strong religious convictions see sections in their children's textbooks that seem to be pushing the ideas of secular humanism, these parents become concerned with the moral ideas that are possibly unconsciously being taught to their children. Likewise then parents with more humanistic views hear of the religious groups protesting the content of particular textbooks, they may feel that these groups are overreacting and may be concerned that textbooks for public schools will become saturated with religious doctrines.

A court case in Mobile, Alabama, presided over by Judge Hand, is one of the best illustrations of this conflict. In this case, six hundred parents and teachers challenged four dozen textbooks used in Alabama because they felt that these books were propagating secular humanism at the expense of traditional religious beliefs. The main argument that these parents and teachers used was that secular humanism is a religion in itself and that because of the laws providing for separation of church and state, it has no business being in a textbook. The defenders stated that secular humanism doesn't exist as a religion and that the only reason these ideas were in the books was to prepare students to enter into our modern world. Finally, on March 4, 1987, Judge Hand ruled that secular humanism is a religion and identified forty-five textbooks that promoted secular humanism. He also insulted the defense by adding that these forty-five textbooks could still be used as reference books for a comparative religion course.

More and more it seems that these cases have become a stage for interest groups to propagate their ideas. The emphasis on removing biases in texts in order to present the student with a balanced view of life seems to be fading. Often cases like these turn into a persuasion match, where both sides spend vast amounts of time trying to convince the opposition to change its mind. As David Underhill reports in his article "Voltaire Arraigned in Alabama: The Textbook Humanism Case," the American Civil Liberties Union (ACLU) and People for the American Way (PAW) came to aid the defense in the case in Mobile. For the plaintiffs, many Baptist churches and even a prominent conservative politician gave their support. Christian and educational television stations ran commercials about this controversy.

Somewhere along the line, parents and teachers have decided that students are not capable of making decisions about what they as young adults feel is right or wrong. It seems that both parties in this case have given textbooks far too much power as influences over young people's lives. Most students I know hardly pay attention to subjects addressed in their texts. Even when they do crack open their books, they certainly aren't going to act out every idea they read about. What have these people in Mobile taught their kids? They've shown them that when they are confronted with ideas that are different from their own they must purge these ideas from the system. To quote Nat Hentoff, a writer concerned about issues that essentially boil down to the issue of our First Amendment rights, the groups in the Mobile case have demonstrated a "lack of faith in the free exchange of ideas."

THE READER'S TURN:

1. To judge from this paper, how serious or significant is the controversy over "secular humanism"?

2. How well do the arguments of the two opposing sides come into focus in this paper? Try to sum up the point of view of each faction in a sentence.

3. After reading this paper, can you write a one-paragraph definition of *secular humanism* that reasonable people on both sides could accept? Try your version out on a small group or on your class as a whole.

4. Where does the writer of this paper stand in relation to the flap over secular humanism? Do you agree with her position? Why or why not?

5. Critics trying to put the finger on what is wrong with the modern world use terms like *materialism, skepticism, relativism, expediency, socialism*. Research the history and uses of one such term; define and illustrate it for the average newspaper reader.

Fundamentalism

I sat with my parents in a small Baptist church in Medina, Texas--my grandfather's church. We were visitors. The young preacher paced up and down before the congregation, his arms flailing about as he spoke. Eventually, he reduced himself to tears, begging those who were repentant to come forward and be saved. Two young women ran crying to him and fell on their knees. The minister laid his hands on their heads and prayed toward the heavens until they were saved. We knew they were saved because he asked them if they had accepted Jesus in their hearts, and they nodded yes.

This place met a need--the need for hope and direction, a need for answers. Huge numbers of us are crammed in cement cities where the crunch of metal, the smell of smog, and the sights of the diseased and homeless surround us. If not living in it, we still see it in even more graphic detail on television where we are harangued with pictures of earthquakes, hurricanes, wars, maimed children, Aids, and serial murders. Then there are the talk shows revealing the dark side of our behavior--the child beating, rape, alcoholism, drug addiction, child pornography, incest, and the list goes on. As we feel powerless over the oppressive mass of negative information, many of us are looking for help, and many are finding it in Fundamentalist religion.

Fundamentalism is a movement among American protestants based on a belief in the Bible as factual historical record an incontrovertible prophecy, including Genesis, the virgin birth, the Second Advent, and Armageddon. "Art's got to preach more from the Bible," the assistant minister of our church said. He was an old-time minister, but his valid observation was that the biggest churches in town were the ones who stuck with the Bible--a literal translation of the Bible. Congregations of tens of thousands go to these enormous churches with budgets in the millions. What is the appeal? People suffering a "fragmented self and shifting desires turn to authoritarian groups to give them the firm direction they hunger for," says Flora Wuellner, minister and author.

This American movement began in the 1830s when a massive social and religious upheaval was going on. A New York farmer predicted, through a literal interpretation of the Bible, the second advent of Christ. There would follow the promised Millennium--a thousand years of peace. The creed as written for the Millenarians in 1878 by James H. Brook was and still is: 1. The verbal inspiration of the Bible--preserving it completely from error in the original manuscript, 2. The Trinity, 3. The total depravity of man, 4. The necessity of a "new birth" for salvation, 5. Substitution atonement, 6. Assurance of salvation to the believer, 7. The premillenial second coming of Christ.

Here's what's wrong, says the creed: man is depraved, and here's how you fix it. You must be reborn through Jesus. And, say the Fundamentalists, this is the only way. This creed has remained through the Millenarians who, after WWI changed their name to Fundamentalists who, after WWII, because of the pejorative association to that name, changed it to Evangelists.

How often hope is based on a better tomorrow! The addict will quit tomorrow, the workaholic will some day get it all done and then be happy, the scientist may work fervently towards that future discovery. "Repent and you will be saved and go to heaven" is the cry of the evangelist. Isn't that the cry of most of our self-help books too? If you do what I tell you, you will be a winner, a better parent, thin, happy, healthy, disease-free, cavity free, a faster runner, richer, more successful, and so on and so on. At the base of this thinking--this grab at a future "something better"--is the idea that we are less than. We must become something we are not. This theme pervades our culture. The preacher's tears--a promise--hope. Hope is what Fundamentalism is all about.

"Life is difficult," Scott Peck, psychiatrist, starts his book The Road Less Travelled. He goes on to explain that spirituality is fundamental to the human solution. The second of his four stages of spirituality is described as having rigid and formalistic behavior, such as a blind commitment to Fundamentalism. Fundamentalists have the formula; they will make it to heaven. The Bible says they will.

THE READER'S TURN:

1. Do you feel the writer of this paper has the right to speak up on this subject? How does she establish her authority or credibility?

2. This topic obviously brings opposing views and contradictory loyalties into play. What rock-bottom historical or factual information does this paper provide?

3. This writer tries to probe the psychological foundations of fundamentalism. What is the gist of her analysis, and how convincing is it?

4. Sum up this writer's definition of fundamentalism. (Would yours have been different?)

5. Apart from overt religious affiliation, what makes a person a Catholic, a Protestant, a Mormon, a Buddhist, or a Puritan? Try to focus on key beliefs and attitudes drawn on first-hand experience and observation.

WRITING TOPICS 5

Many people have heard terms like *Oedipus complex* or *fascist* but would not recognize one if they met one in broad daylight. Other people make derogatory remarks about liberals but do not know enough about what true liberals stand for or believe in. Slogans like *law and order* are often too much like blank checks—we don't know exactly what we sign for when we endorse them. Definition fills our readers in on what we mean. It keeps words from being empty words or empty promises or a mere smokescreen to mask a hidden agenda.

1. Types and Stereotypes: What's a Yankee? What's a redneck? What's a yuppie? What is the stereotype, and is there any truth in it? (Is there a New York City type? Is there a California mentality?)

2. Fighting Words: What's an elitist (and what's wrong with being one)? Are we living in a patriarchal society? What do women mean when they say: "I'm not a feminist, but..."? Are all males by definition sexist? Is American education inherently racist? Focus on one such term—its legitimate meaning and uses.

3. Americana: Many young Americans study American history at a stage in their growing up when their minds are on something else. Suppose you are trying to fill them in on one of the key concepts or key forces in American history that they may have missed. Write a paper that will bring to life for them a term like *populism, the frontier, abolitionist, nonconformist, laissez-faire, assimilation.*

4. Cultural Literacy: Critics of American education are complaining that in today's classrooms allusions to "what every educated person knows" often draw only blank stares. To help make your contemporaries culturally literate, define and bring to life a term like the following: *Oedipus complex, Renaissance man, Puritanism, mysticism, surrealism, territorial imperative, art nouveau.*

5. New Wave: Often we know about current trends only at second hand. Can you serve as an expert guide to a current trend or new wave? What is genuine *nouvelle cuisine*? What is collaborative learning? What is androgyny? What is today's ideal career woman? Use contrast with more conventional alternatives to help you define and illustrate your key term.

6
Argument: Pro and Con

The purpose of a logical argument is to take the reader along step by step to the right conclusion. The basic assumption underlying such an argument is that rational people can look at the evidence together without letting bias or emotion cloud their judgment. When you present a logical argument, you try to help the reader think the matter through. You try to show by what process of reasoning you arrived at the stand you take on an issue.

An excellent way to keep from jumping to conclusions is to weigh the pro and con and lead the reader to a balanced end result. This kind of argument leaves both writer and reader better informed because it makes them look at more than one side of an issue. It helps writers avoid the temptation to brush off opposing arguments or to treat people who disagree with them as half-wits or people of ill will. Look at the way the following student papers systematically line up advantages and disadvantages or strong and weak points.

Motorcycle Helmets

In this genuine pro-and-con paper, the writer shows that he understands and sympathizes with both sides—and yet arrives at a strong conclusion, taking a strong stand at the end.

The *Goldene Medinah*

How much immigration is too much? On a subject clouded by emotion and special pleading, this writer sorts out the arguments for and against, showing why it is hard to demonstrate a clear mandate for a change in current policy.

Drugs on the Job

Taking up the controversial subject of drug testing, this writer presents strong arguments on both sides but finally takes a clear-cut stand after giving full consideration to difficulties and doubts.

Whose Right to Life?

With emotions on the subject of abortion running high on both sides, this writer tries to give at least a polite hearing to the pro-Life arguments but soon comes out strongly for pro-Choice.

Home Care or Institutional Care?

This writer tries to do an honest soul-searching on a topic that is fraught with potential heartache and that leaves little room for easy answers.

Motorcycle Helmets

We have a problem. Too many people die in motorcyle accidents who could be saved if they wore helmets. I say "we" even though I don't drive a motorcycle and have no intention of starting. I do, however, have friends who are motorcyle riders and a colleague who has lost a son to a motorcycle accident. What appears simple--putting on a helmet to protect oneself against a death-threatening injury--isn't the only issue. I understand riders who prefer to go without headgear. I drive a convertible because I love that feeling of freedom--the openness and the feel of the wind in my hair.

My friends who ride motorcycles and choose not to wear helmets have several good reasons for not doing so and I agree with them all. They believe their cycle to be one of the last vestiges of real freedom available in an urban society. The motorcycle rider is the modern cowboy, and no self-respecting rider would be found wearing anything more protective than a Stetson. To force a plastic helmet that effectively shuts out the outdoors is unthinkable.

Another argument is that a helmet reduces the riders' ability to hear what is going on around them. The better the helmet, the less they can hear, they maintain, and that's important when road noises such as sirens and horn honking by other drivers are important indicators of events happening around them. Many say that peripheral vision is also limited by today's Star-Trek-styled contraptions.

An additional concern is the cost. A good quality helmet with protective face mask costs in the neighborhood of $60 and change. That is, if you'll settle for the minimum, which many riders would opt for if helmets were required. Many motorcyclists, especially students, choose this form of transportation because it is inexpensive. Some simply can't pay the sixty-plus dollars to conform with a law they never supported.

Storage of helmet--when not riding, and away from home--is another problem. Helmets, today, are astronaut-like affairs constructed of plastic, steel, and foam far larger than the rider's head. Few cycles are equipped with a storage container sufficient to hold the helmet securely. The rider is faced with the dilemma of taking the bulky headpiece with him or leaving an expensive item out in the open subject to theft.

I not only understand and empathize with these points --I agree with them. My contention is that the reasons for wearing a helmet are also convincing.

Statistics indicate that 20,000 lives could be spared each year in the U.S. if cyclists wore protective headgear. That's a lot of sons and daughters and brothers and sisters.

In California, 86% of the medical costs associated with motorcycle injuries are ultimately borne by the state. That indicates that many cyclists have inadequate (or non-existent) insurance to cover their own injuries or lack the resources to finance their own care.

California, like many other states, recently passed a mandatory seatbelt law requiring every driver and passenger in an automobile to wear a seatbelt or other safety restraining device such as a secured baby seat. Many drivers ignore the law, but increasing numbers are complying in spite of the discomfort and freedom-of-movement concerns shared by cycle riders. This isn't a "what's good for the goose is good for the gander too" issue. Auto drivers don't want their two-wheeled brethren of the road to be forced into equally restrictive protection just because they are suddenly belted by law. The point is, some laws provide benefits that outweigh their shortcomings. Seatbelt laws for motorists and helmet laws for cyclists are examples.

Motorcyclists are disadvantaged from the start. They all admit it. Auto drivers are surrounded by two tons of steel and iron. Automakers pride themselves on their ability to make their products stronger, better engineered, and more "crash-proof." In anything but the worst highway situations, the car driver survives even serious accidents. Not so with cyclists. Motorcyclists, inherently, are no more safe now than before safety became an issue. Right or wrong, fault or no fault, the motorcyclist remains extremely vulnerable. Given even a medium speed confrontation between an auto and a cycle the outcome becomes morbidly predictable--especially if the cyclist is helmetless. This disparity of size, weight and bulk isn't likely to change so why not protect oneself as much as possible?

Everyone who is concerned with the issue of helmets required for motorcyclists by law is aware of the arguments presented here. Even so, I believe the reasons for wearing a helmet (maintaining the life of <u>numero uno</u>) outweigh the freedom of rejecting restrictive headgear. Still, there remains one other argument.

A year ago a motorcyclist hit the rear fender of my car and severely mangled his right foot. The accident wasn't my fault, but I remain distraught at the thought of a young man maimed as the result of an accident that I survived simply because of all that steel protection. He was wearing a helmet and tennis shoes. As a result, his foot was broken--not his head.

The foot healed quickly and life went ahead. Had that young man been killed, I would be tormented to this day. Anyone would. Fault or no-fault, one does not forget nor totally forgive such an incident.

I can't live with the thought of a motorcyclist dying beneath the wheels of my automobile. Right or wrong-- fault or no-fault--I don't want the image of your tangled body and scrambled brains cluttering the roadway of my consciousness for the rest of my life.

THE READER'S TURN:

1. The natural instinct of writers with strong opinions is to go all out to destroy the opposition. This writer takes a very different tack. Show how this paper meets people with opposing views halfway.

2. Outline the arguments and counter-arguments in pro and con style. Which seem most real or most convincing?

3. The author of this paper is a journalism student who is exceptionally audience-conscious. Look especially at the introduction and the concluding paragraphs. What does the writer do to involve the reader? Why and with what effect does the writer save the last argument till the end?

4. Cars and motorcycles are not just means of transportation. They serve as symbols or satisfy psychological needs. What role does this assumption play in this paper? What supporting evidence can you cite from your own experience or observation?

5. Proposals designed to improve safety or traffic flow are often hotly debated. Explore the pros and cons of a currently debated proposal or scheme: airbags, special lanes for car pools or buses, light rail systems for urban transport, escort systems for students in evening classes. Push toward a reasonable conclusion.

The *Goldene Medinah*

America has traditionally been a land of immigrants. Our history books usually begin with the immigration of English settlers in the 17th century. Most Americans are descended from one of the subsequent waves of immigrants from Germany or Italy or China or other countries. To millions of Jewish immigrants, America was the goldene medinah--the promised golden shore. Of course, immigration can cause problems, and American policies toward immigration have reflected this in their vacillation between "open door" and "closed door" policies. In the seventies alone, 11 million new immigrants came to this country. Such high immigration rates are making us ask the question: Should America restrict further immigration?

The primary arguments against immigration are economic. Immigrants add to the available supply of labor, thus bringing down wages. Since they are usually willing to settle for a lower standard of living, they may take jobs that would otherwise have gone to Americans asking higher wages. This argument was the basis of a recent Immigration and Naturalization Service (INS) campaign, called "Operation Jobs," aiming at removing aliens working illegally from their jobs and deporting them, thus freeing those jobs for American workers.

Immigrants may receive benefits at the expense of the government and taxpayers. They receive assistance for the first six months of their residence; and afterwards, they may be eligible for welfare or unemployment benefits. Immigrants and their children benefit from free schooling. With all the recent drastic cuts in assistance programs, it seems we can hardly take care of the American poor, let alone immigrants.

Continued immigration may deprive our children and grandchildren of their share of resources. America's land and physical resources are limited. When America's founders arrived, they believed that the forests were so extensive that they could never be depleted. So they logged and cleared, and in less than two centuries, the forests are a fraction of their former size. Similarly, it appears to us that there is plenty of land for both immigrants and residents. But if we continue to readily accept immigrants, we will necessarily limit the amount of resources available for our descendants.

While small numbers of immigrants tend to become Americanized, large numbers of immigrants from one country tend to maintain their old customs, without learning new ones. I once worked in a restaurant located near an area with a concentration of Spanish-speaking people. I had extreme difficulty dealing with these people, many of whom did not speak any English.

But there are also arguments favoring immigration. The kinds of jobs that immigrants take are often low-paying, low-prestige jobs. In the last century, Chinese and Irish people were encouraged to immigrate to work on the railroads--low-paying, backbreaking work. Between 1945 and 1960, <u>braceros</u> were brought from Mexico to work in the farms and fields. More recent immigrants may be found picking fruit or plucking chickens or sanding down furniture. In a recent roundup of illegal immigrants, 21 workers were removed from one poultry processing plant; of the 12 people hired to replace them, half quit within three days. Without immigrants, these jobs might not be filled at all.

And if immigrants are earning money here, they also spend it here. Immigrants, like everyone else, buy food, clothing, homes, and cars. Working immigrants pay their share in taxes. And while they may keep wages down, that implies that they keep prices down too.

While the mixture of cultures brought about by immigration can create problems, it can also create a vital diversity. Restaurants specializing in Mexican or Vietnamese or German or other ethnic foods are popular with Americans of all cultural backgrounds. The festivities of the Chinese New Year and the Cinco de Mayo are enjoyed by many, not just Chinese or Mexicans. Inner-city neighborhoods that were once given up for dead are now bustling with the colorful life of Little Saigon or Hong Kong West.

Traditionally, immigrants have often been the most patriotic Americans. The letters Polish Americans or Vietnamese Americans write to the Old Country are often more effective than any propaganda by the voice of America. It is clear we cannot accept everyone who wishes to immigrate. At the same time, immigrants can make valuable contributions to America, and our immigration laws should reflect this fact. The best immigration policy is one similar to our current policy: to keep a watchful eye on the total numbers but to allow the dynamism created by large numbers of immigrants willing to work and eager to succeed.

THE READER'S TURN:

1. What kind of audience would care about this topic one way or the other? Who are possible readers who might be expected to listen to these arguments?

2. Outline the arguments pro and con. Do they become real or convincing? Do any of them seem pale or far-fetched? Which seem strongest to you?

3. What are this writer's sources? Trace the mix of personal experience, current media coverage, and historical information in this paper.

4. Pro and con papers sometimes end inconclusively, leaving the reader confused or undecided. Does this paper build to a strong or satisfying conclusion? Does it leave you with a lasting overall impression?

5. Is the idea of a "nation of immigrants" more than a cliché for you? What is your first hand experience with immigrants, immigration, or opposition to it? Do you have any feelings pro or con?

Drugs on the Job

The 6,700 employees of the night shift at General Motors were busy assembling Oldsmobiles and Buicks when ten police officers rushed into the factory and handcuffed twelve workers who had apparently sold illicit drugs including cocaine, hashish, LSD, and marijuana to two undercover agents hired by G.M. California Edison Co. organized its own raid, after receiving a tip, where corporate managers and security officers searched through 400 employee lockers, checked cars in the parking lot, and went as far as to ask a few workers to empty out their pockets. Seven employees were fired for possessing drugs or alcohol at work in violation of company rules. Employers are fighting back and sending out a message: They want a drug-free environment. Hundreds of companies are setting up programs to combat drugs by using urinalysis to identify the users. Mandatory drug testing has been a controversial issue, a matter that needs to be addressed. However, concerns ranging from costs, search and seizure rights, to inaccurate findings are just a few snags complicating this problem.

The increase of illegal drugs has become a major problem among blue and white collar workers alike. Federal experts estimate that ten to twenty-three percent of all U.S. workers use dangerous drugs on the job. In order to secure a drug-free workplace, adopting a mandatory drug testing program may be the one answer, especially in highly sensitive areas, such as transportation, public service, power plants, to name a few.

Drug abuse on the job is draining the energy, reliability, and the integrity of our labor force in America. According to the Research Triangle Institute, drug abuse costs the U.S. economy $60 billion in a single year. For example, a computer operator high on marijuana failed to load a crucial tape into an American Airlines computer reservations system. The system was out of service for eight hours, costing the company some $19 million. Other studies show that drug users are far less productive than their coworkers, miss ten times as many workdays, and are three times as likely to injure themselves or someone else besides costing the employer an enormous amount of money. Weeding out the drug users by means of drug testing seems to be the answer; unfortunately, others feel differently. The invasion of privacy has become a central issue.

The Fourth Amendment spells out the right of the people to be secure in their persons, houses, papers, and effects against unreasonable searches and seizures. It was written for our protection. But since possessing illegal drugs is unlawful, this amendment would not necessarily apply. If company policy states that there will be no use of illegal drugs on the job, then the employee should expect some type of drug test program, especially if the welfare of the public is involved.

Inaccurate drug test readings have been another concern. Lewis L. Maltby, vice-president at Drexelbrook Engineering, says the most common type of testing has been shown to have false positive results: "Clean" samples are mistakenly labeled as "dirty" 20% to 30% of the time. An inaccurate result may have all kinds of ramifications, such as loss of job or even a lawsuit against the company. According to an article in <u>Newsweek</u>, test procedures used carelessly can produce a finding for marijuana when the urine contains ibuprofen, the basic anti-inflammatory ingredient in many widely used over-the-counter pain relievers. Deliberate altering of tests is another problem. Drug-abusing employees who are not watched can switch with someone who is clean, or dilute urine with tap water that reduces drug concentration to below the cutoff point. The only way to prevent cheating on the test is to make the employee strip at the waist and be observed. Of course this is humiliating, and the right of privacy is violated.

There is also the question of the high cost of drug testing. According to the Federal Commission, it would cost $45 per person, which could run into millions. However, drug abuse in this country is costing us billions, so we can't afford not to test for drugs in the workplace. Once we find the users, they could be given an opportunity to be rehabilitated and treated. The main objective is to find the users and help them with their problem.

We have to remember that drug testing is for the safety and welfare of the public. Since 1975 there have been fifty train accidents leaving 37 deaths, 80 injured, and $34 million in damage. In New Jersey two crewmen died when a cargo jet skidded off the runway. The autopsy found the pilot had been high on marijuana. Thirty workers in a nuclear power plant had drug charges filed against them four years ago. In the case of a nuclear accident, these workers have to respond quickly or the consequences could be devastating. The safety of the public needs to be a number-one priority.

I recently had a conversation with a man in his sixties about drug testing on the job. We talked at length about the subject, and he agreed that drug testing would be a good idea. He had recently been going through some medical treatment for cancer and had been put on drugs for the pain. He said his mind was definitely affected by the drugs and his doctor still hadn't given him permission to drive his vehicle. He said his logical thinking processes had been impaired. He knew firsthand how drugs have altered his reactions. With that, I too was convinced that drugs whether prescribed or taken illegally can cause side effects. I have come to a clear conclusion that mandatory drug testing for sensitive positions is a logical approach to our drug problem in the workplace today, and for the welfare and safety of the public it is a must.

THE READER'S TURN:

1. What makes this topic an especially explosive or controversial issue? Who are some of the people likely to care most?
2. When charges and counter-charges fly, we gladly turn to a writer furnishing detailed factual information and staying close to concrete examples. Where and how does this paper use concrete examples and factual details?
3. How would you sum up the basic arguments pro and con? Do you think the writer presents them with an open mind?
4. Do you agree with the writer's conclusion? Why or why not? How do you justify your own stand?
5. We are often torn when we have to choose between individual rights and the greater good of society. For instance, we may find it difficult to choose between the right to privacy and the right of the police to search for evidence of crime. We may find it hard to choose between protecting the privacy of people with disabling or infectious illnesses and warning others of possible hazards. Explore both sides of one such difficult choice.

Whose Right to Life?

The word <u>abortion</u> typically brings up strong images in everyone's mind. For some, the image will be of dead fetuses, thrown without dignity into dumpsters behind clinics. For others, it means throngs of people harassing and beating women seeking aid, and in the South it also conjures images of clinic bombings, an act of blatant terrorism. Weeding out the emotions from the arguments is necessary before a decision can be made.

In 1973, the Supreme Court was confronted with the still controversial case of Roe vs. Wade. In a 7-2 vote, the justices decided to allow women the right of abortion on demand within the first six months of pregnancy. The decision invalidated laws in Texas and Georgia and overturned restrictive legislation in 44 states. Since then, the number of abortions has climbed, peaking in the early 1980's. In 1973, more than 745,000 abortions were performed. Ten years later, more than 1,200,000 were performed. Not only had the number nearly doubled, but the number of women per thousand who had had abortions had also nearly doubled. The court case ended the rash of illegal abortions performed under circumstances dangerous to both doctors and patients, but it opened up a chasm between two rigorously lobbying political groups: the Right-to-Life group and the Pro-Choice group.

The proponents of Right-to-Life regard the fetus as a human being with all its rights. They point to the Constitution and say, " The founders of this country intended that no one's rights be abridged by any other. How can we deny rights to a group simply because they can't speak for themselves?" Many base the argument on religious grounds. They cite the Ten Commandments and say, "Thou shall not kill." They may believe that the soul enters the body at conception and that abortion denies God's will for the potential child. Religious leaders have attempted to make their fight appeal to the secular community as well. In a forum on a PBS Frontline special, evangelist Pat Robertson said that abortion and birth control "deny this country potential taxpayers." As an alternative, the Right-to-Life movement offers adoption and federal welfare programs for poor mothers.

On the other hand, the Pro-Choice lobby has protected the Roe vs. Wade decision by claiming a woman's right to control her body without state interference. To them a fetus is simply a group of cells and, as such, has no rights as a human. The fetus has no more rights than a burst appendix or cancer cells. Some women are at serious health risk from pregnancy. Carrying a child may complicate some forms of muscle disease and heart trouble, as well as other ailments. In such a case, death may result to mother and fetus.

In addition, the woman may suffer emotional scars if her pregnancy is the result of rape or incest. She may lose opportunities as well. Many high schools ban pregnant students from attending mainstream classes. Although schooling is offered to teenage mothers, the subjects taught usually cover little more than childrearing, as was the case at my old high school. Lack of education and insufficient finances are only the beginning of a lifelong struggle with poverty for many women. For these reasons, Pro-Choice people do not see adoption and welfare assistance as options for all women. Most importantly, abortion is not thrust upon its opponents. The opponents are not forced to practice abortion. What the Right-to-Life people protest, the Pro-Choice people say, is others' right to choose.

    Ultimately, the right to choose her own options must be any woman's prerogative. Her wish and hers alone must be considered. Although at later stages of pregnancy the fetus may be considered a child, the Roe vs. Wade decision covers only the first six months. Moreover, most women abort considerably before the second trimester. Ninety percent of abortions are performed by the end of the third month, and less than one percent abort at the fifth month. Right-to-Life people point out that the fetus is a potential life, but a potential is not an actual. Denying women the right to abort subordinates the life of the woman to the potential life of the fetus, subjugates the real to the possible. The primary objection to abortion is based on religious grounds, and this makes a ruling in favor of the Right-to-Life a breach of the constitutional law that separates state and religion. A religious woman with whom I spoke as a young teen made a lasting impression on me when she sniffed, "These young girls who sleep around deserve what they get. They should pay for their sins." My heart still aches at the thought that she would think of sex as a criminal act and that she would consider a child punishment rather than joy. In my late teens, I accompanied a friend having an abortion. Her boyfriend had abandoned her when she discovered that she was pregnant. She had gone through all of the options with a counselor at Planned Parenthood before she had chosen abortion. They advised her conscientiously, never pushing her one way and always explaining what she could expect at each decision. As I waited in the clinic to drive my friend home, I looked around to see that the others waiting for the same reason were also women. I thought how nature saddled women alone with this responsibility of gestation, childbearing, and nursing. Men may care and help: They may make mercenary marriages, or they may pay child support. But without control over their bodies and knowledge of their options, women are slaves to their reproductive systems.

THE READER'S TURN:

1. Are you tired of the issue of abortion? Do you think there is any point in further discussion of the issue?

2. The writer starts by saying that "weeding out the emotions" is necessary before a decision can be make. Does she succeed? Does this paper sketch out some basic facts that both sides should be able to agree on?

3. Has this writer succeeded in listening to those on the other side? Do you think she presents their arguments fairly?

4. How effectively does this writer present her own position? Does the effectiveness of her argument depend on her audience? Do you think her appeal to solidarity among women will be effective with most female readers?

5. Where do *you* stand on this issue? Which of the arguments pro and con do you think are most important? Which sway you most?

Homecare or Institutional Care?

America is increasingly becoming a nation of elderly people; 29% in 1986, with a projected yearly increase through the end of the century. As a result, more and more people with elderly parents or spouses must make the decision whether to care for them at home or confine them to a "home." The decision is especially difficult for those people with relatives who suffer from Alzheimer's and other debilitating diseases.

Proponents of in-home care cite a variety of reasons for their preference. Growing old can be a disorienting and disquieting process for many people. The individual who grows old gracefully is atypical; many more elderly find that their decreased physical and mental abilities are a source of embarrassment and frustration. If one has to be helped to the bathroom, hand-fed, dressed and bathed, isn't it better to have someone you know and love assisting than a detached stranger?

For years institutions for the elderly, or "homes," have had a negative connotation. Images of uncaring workers, dirty facilities, and demoralizing treatment prevent many people from committing their relatives to such places. There is a sense that in-home care provides the elderly person with a more dignified form of care. Isn't it better that only our families see our decline? We can retain some pride by being, at least outwardly, more independent. No one else has to know that we are beset with humiliating weaknesses in our twilight years.

In addition to the security and dignity issues, home-care can be financially less expensive than institutional care. Institutional care can amount to $2000 a month and up, depending upon the demands of the elderly person's condition. Federal aid is virtually nonexistent for anyone who has any assets at all. Savings and major assets such as homes must be liquidated and expended before the government will adequately assist someone facing institutional expenses. In order to circumvent governmental regulations, many people must seek legal counsel which in itself can be costly and demoralizing. An elderly spouse who must consider spending a lifetime's savings in support of her elderly partner may feel the burden too great to bear alone. For the family of an elderly person, the legalities and expense of institutional care often seem insurmountable and in-home care the only option.

Finally, the prospect of "imprisoning" and "abandoning" a loved one to an institution creates such guilt for the caregiver that it is no longer an option. Even for a family with an incontinent old person, the few glints of lucidity that person may have may be enough to dissuade the family from institutional care. After all, mightn't the old person feel abandoned or unloved during his small flashes of reality? How would we feel being left to die in a sterile environment with many "old people," where no one cares about us?

On the other hand, institutional care provides the elderly person with an educated and specialized staff who are committed to their work. The institution can dispense medication, provide emergency care, and provide the individual with an environment that is designed to meet the needs of the elderly. The in-home care giver might not be adequately educated to deal effectively with an emergency, nor might he have the ability to provide adequate nutrition or medication. Some elderly people become violent or wander away from home. An institution can better cope with this type of situation than can the individual.

Institutional caregivers are generally compassionate individuals who view their charges with respect. The institutional caregiver is not burdened with the emotional baggage of seeing a loved one decline and become dependent. The infirmities of the old person are not viewed negatively, but as a normal part of the aging process. My own grandfather who suffered from Alzheimer's, carried a bottle of suppositories with him, could not eat without help, and had no control of his bowels; but he remained physically strong and determined to carry out his own will no matter how irrational. For my mother and grandmother, this decline was a source of despair, anger, and frustration. The paternal head of the family, a man of power and physical presence, was reduced to a drooling, incapacitated "vegetable." Yet for his institutional caregivers, he was merely another patient who needed their care, no more and no less. They did not feel the betrayal and grief that we did.

Finally, marriages and careers can be ruined by in-home care. Generally, one person must become the sole caregiver for the elderly person. This may result in a loss of time with other family members, suspension of a career, and the stress involved in role changing responsibilities associated with caring for an elderly relative. Institutional care, however, allows the family of the elderly to have a more continuous lifestyle. Of course the stress related to having an elderly relative is not diminished merely because that individual is institutionalized. But the fact that the individual is being cared for outside of the home gives the illusion that everything within the home is normal. The conditions within the household remain fairly constant.

The choice, then, whether to institutionalize or offer in-home care to the needy elderly person is a difficult one. Both choices have benefits and liabilities for the individual and his relatives. But there is no better time to discuss the options than before the decision is really necessary. By considering all the ramifications before the fact, we will be better able to cope with the situation when it arises.

THE READER'S TURN:

1. This paper deals with the kind of subject that many people try to put out of mind. Does the writer succeed in making you care? Why or why not?
2. Does this paper proceed in true "on the one hand" and "on the other hand" fashion? What are the major arguments, and do they seem equally balanced?
3. How much of this paper is theory, and how much is based on firsthand observation or experience? Is there a "personal connection"?
4. Both the introduction and conclusion stay on a fairly general and impersonal level. Are they too colorless and indecisive? Or are they effective as they are?
5. Do you share the bias of those for whom institutions have "a negative connotation"? Why or why not?

WRITING TOPICS 6

We often feel that people around us reach conclusions or make decisions without having thought the matter through. We may then try to argue with them. Like *Star Trek*'s Mr. Spock, we try to make their thinking more logical; we try to make them listen to reason. Try your hand at putting together a step-by-step argument that will take your readers along to a logical conclusion.

1. Choices: Help your readers make up their minds about a choice that they may sooner or later confront. Give them three good reasons why they should

   - get married (or stay single)
   - go to work (or stay in school)
   - enlist (or stay out of the army)
   - buy a Japanese car (or buy American)
   - give money for missionary work (or button their purses)
   - vote in the next election (or sit it out)
   - support student government (or write it off as irrelevant)
   - stay married (or get divorced)
   - plan to have children (or not)

2. Standing on Principle: Do you ever find yourself saying: "It's the principle of the thing"? Take a stand on an issue where you feel an important principle is at stake. Explain and defend the principle and show how it applies to the issue at hand. Choose a topic like drug testing, prison furloughs, testing of drunk drivers, faculty supervision of student publications, car pool lanes, "sin taxes" on tobacco or alcohol, recruitment scandals, or preferential hiring of minorities.

3. Trend Watchers: We often hear experts make confident generalizations about a current trend—only to see them challenged or questioned by other experts. Is it true that people on social security are relatively well off? Is it true that homelessness is growing by leaps and bounds? Is it true that today's students care mostly about jobs and money? Is it true that almost any sophisticated gadget or device we buy is made overseas? Is it true that many teachers in the public schools are demoralized? Try to test one such generalization and revise it as necessary. Draw on statistics, first-hand observations, interviews. Pile up convincing evidence to support your own confirmed or revised generalization.

4. Pro and Con: On difficult decisions, we often need to sift the arguments pro and con. Often we need to balance off advantages and disadvantages, benefits and undesirable side effects. Look at the pro and con concerning a much debated initiative or course of action. You may want to focus on a specific proposal or practice, like banning handguns, requiring motorcycle helmets, changing a course from a lecture format to small-group discussions, allowing parents to bring small children to the workplace or classroom, or turning downtown streets into a pedestrian mall. Aim at a balanced conclusion.

5. Keeping Your Cool: Arguments often get heated, generating more warmth than light. Have you been close to an argument or controversy that has made tempers flare up? Do you feel there has been too much personal animosity, self-righteousness, prejudice, or name-calling? Write a paper designed to calm everyone's temper and to refocus discussion on relevant facts and underlying issues.

7
Persuasion: The Power of Words

All effective writing has an impact on the reader. An effective piece of writing can make us think; it may make us see the other side; it may change our outlook or affect an important choice. We put an article or a paper under the heading of persuasion when changing the reader's mind or ways becomes the writer's overriding goal.

Persuasive writing takes aim squarely at the audience; it tries to bring the reader around. Sometimes we can judge its effectiveness by a practical result: a vote, a sale, a change of policy, a decision overturned. At other times we can see its power to break down resistance, to enlist support for a cause, or to convert people to a new way of thinking.

The following student papers illustrate some of the strategies and challenges of persuasive writing:

For the Sake of Appearances

The first task of the persuasive writer is to get the reader's attention. This writer knows how to make us listen, how to arouse our concern. Looking at the plight of the homeless from a new and provocative perspective, this paper appeals to the conscience of the jaded and apathetic reader.

The Strong and the Rugged

A basic traditional strategy of the persuasive writer is to come on strong—to be assertive, to make strong charges in order to make people re-examine and change their ways. This writer mounts a frontal attack on the media-perpetuated ideal of the macho male.

Marriage: Bond or Bondage?

An alternative strategy for effective persuasion is to meet the readers halfway—to listen to and respect their concerns. This writer listens respectfully to the reservations many young people today have about marriage—and then tries to change their minds.

Justice

Readers tire of hearing the same familiar arguments for or against capital punishment or abortion—arguments which do not seem to change the outlook of the contending factions. This writer breaks through the cliché barrier by looking at the issue of capital punishment from an entirely new and unexpected perspective.

Go in Peace

Ultimately the test of our power to persuade is our attempt to champion an unpopular view. This writer makes a strong plea designed to cause us to re-examine traditional objections to "mercy killing."

For the Sake of Appearances

As the Eighties advance, the plight of the homeless is emerging as one of the most disturbing social dilemmas of our time. The treatment the homeless are receiving in general is tragic enough, but insupportable is the way they are being dealt with in cities with a show to put on.

During the last year, we have witnessed some striking examples of cities brushing the "dirt" under the rug as they prepared for a major media event. While the immediate effect of the event is to put the cities "on the map," the corresponding bad press that is generated from the callous treatment of the homeless is certainly not attractive. The ultimate effect, as the cities subordinate humanity to appearances, is one of shallowness and hypocrisy.

In 1987, San Francisco was chosen as one of the larger North American cities to host Pope John Paul on his New World sojourn. Months before the event, city officials embarked upon a massive clean-up operation. Hundreds of thousands of dollars were allocated from public and private funds to put a shiny face on the California mecca of sophistication and home to thousands of the faithful. To prepare for this historic visit it was necessary to cut a pristine swath through the city to accommodate the Pope's motorcade, and to beautify all sights the Pope was scheduled to behold. Cleaning up the streets required polishing buildings and other public places; sprucing up the living landscape meant planting, mowing, trimming, and doing something about the troublesome bodies "littering" the sidewalks of the inner city.

What to do, then, with the forgotten ones? Among these unfortunate people were the former inmates of state mental hospitals carelessly and erroneously deemed capable of reentering a society that had no place for them. Included, too, were the wanderers--men and women, each with sad and unique stories, but all jobless, whose common home was the streets of San Francisco.

The resolution of this problem was the <u>temporary</u> displacement of these unfortunate people to flop-houses and shelters, then back to the streets when the Pope departed. What the operation amounted to was a cover-up of a tragic situation that doesn't go away that easily. How much more life-confirming it would have been if the funds designated to impress the Pope were used instead to house, feed, and rehabilitate the homeless, if only for a short time. And how ironic that these appearances were created for one called an emissary of Christ, champion of the unloved and forgotten of the world.

A year later, the forgotten were again suddenly recalled as two other American cities prepared to have the eyes of the world upon them.

In June of 1988, the city of Atlanta was gearing up for the Democratic National Convention. But days before any gavel struck wood or balloons were released, the television cameras had focused in on an area of potential civic sensitivity. It seemed that the main route that delegates and guests would travel from hotels to convention hall passed by a particularly embarrassing section where the homeless had constructed a shanty-town of sorts. Cardboard shelters under bridges and make-shift "homes" fashioned from the detritus of an affluent society were strung along this route, soon to be highly visible to the visitors converging on Atlanta from forty-nine other states. The solution this time was another stop-gap measure, seemingly humane but ultimately cruel. Temporary apartments were hastily outfitted as dormitories--supplied with beds, clean linen, and even food in the refrigerators. Meanwhile the offending shelters were removed from sight. When the last cheer had sounded and the delegates were back on their planes, the displaced would be returned to their old haunts, attempting to restore their pitiful domesticity.

By August and the Republican National convention in New Orleans, no spark had caught flame. The increasingly familiar pre-event focus by the news media found officials coming up with the same tired solutions: get them out of sight while the city tastes its hour of glory.

These measures to preserve appearances at the expense of the homeless impose a stain upon otherwise joyous events: the historic visit of a Pope to our area, the uniquely American hoopla of political conventions.

Inadvertently, these media events revealed more than intended--that the homeless are regarded by many civic authorities as an embarrassment. What is significant is that so much energy and resourcefulness can be mounted so quickly to get the homeless to disappear temporarily, while so little is done by government on a day-to-day basis to alleviate their plight.

THE READER'S TURN:

1. How does this writer make us take a new look at a familiar problem? How is this paper different from what you might expect in the usual newspaper story about the homeless?

2. The writer has strategically selected key examples. The first example, dealing with the visit of the Pope, seemed to her particularly "ironic." What does she mean? How well-deserved is her irony?

3. Persuasive writers persist, keeping after the reader. What is the effect of the writer's following through with her two additional examples? How are they parallel to the first; how are they different?

4. Indictments of "shallowness and hypocrisy" may shame some people but may make others hostile. Which of the two do you think is the most likely result to be produced by this paper? How did it affect you?

5. Modern observers have often looked with a skeptical or ironic eye at celebrations, ceremonies, or civic events. How do *you* feel about them? Debate the pro and con, focusing on one or more test cases or striking examples.

The Strong and the Rugged

Appearances sometimes do not lie. The media have consistently perpetuated portrayals of men as macho: dirty, hairy, mute, rough and tough characters. Clint Eastwood, for example, does not ask questions, but shoots to kill first. He is a man of few words in his movies. He is usually unshaved with a dirty, craggy face, and his clothes consist of only one outfit and are never clean. Other male macho movie stars can even have a large gross scar made up on their face to show how really tough they can be in both enduring pain and integrating this pain into their persons. These macho type males are consistently beating each other's faces bloody and then walking away to have a cold brew. Causing pain has become a national pastime sport on television. A neurosurgeon once shared with me the fact that these men who beat each other have an enormous amount of incurred brain damage. I have often been curious as to how much brain damage existed before they started beating each other.

Sadly enough, our male children sit in front of their televisions and grow up seeing these behaviors as manly, adult models for them to imitate in their adult lives. They want guns, cowboy hats, and boxing gloves for Christmas presents. They spend their teenage years at the video booths killing objects, sometimes people on the screen. Surprisingly enough, their parents are willing to promote this type of behavior in the cause of bringing their boys up to be rough and tough too. The parents themselves are impressed with these strong, silent brutes who entertain them in their nice, clean, civilized suburban homes. Some years ago, this type of male image won Clint Eastwood the mayoral election in Carmel, California. If at any time Mayor Eastwood did not agree with his political opposition, he could always shoot them. President Reagan was first promoted to voters through the media as a strong man of few words, a rough and tough type of cowboy. People again voted for this type of manly image to solve their nation's domestic and foreign affairs.

Macho has influenced the lives of the majority of the people in our society. We have learned that appearances, however, are the least of our problems. I will discuss and show examples of how macho behavior has become dangerous in human relationships, how I have personally been affected by this behavior, and how professional testing and research confirm that certain important characteristics and emotional qualities are lacking in the more macho, highly masculine man.

The emotional and mental makeup of individuals is of primary importance in their ability to exhibit healthy interactions with the rest of society. Men who are so easily disconnected from their feelings are not only capable of shooting before asking questions, but are also capable of raping their daughters, killing innocent children, beating their wives, killing animals for the sport of it, and laying waste to the environment around them. These kinds of acts are often attributed to the macho man, who uses violence and dominance to control or feel secure in his environment.

Macho is a dirty word for me. As a woman I feel these threats in a very real personal way. For instance, I cannot go out of my house after dark without the fear of being possibly attacked either verbally or physically by a man who feels he must invade my freedom to move. I cannot enjoy the wilderness alone or go camping for the same reasons. I belong to a health club where I pay good money, probably to a man, to go swim and relax in the sauna and hot tub. Often I find myself having to tell some big he-man to stop staring at me. He has no idea he is being intrusive to my person.

There is current professional research and testing showing that these behaviors are attributed to the macho, more masculine man and that these behaviors hinder the man's ability to relate to other people. A psychologist named Sandra Lipsitz Bem, a professional at Stanford University, ran a series of experiments on college students who had been categorized as highly masculine men. The results of the tests showed that these men scored painfully low in their degree of nurturance--warmth and caring for others in humane situations. These same men were also the least supportive and least responsive in an experiment requiring these attributes.

Lack of warmth and caring for other people, children, animals and nature has become increasingly threatening to our society. There is a need to change this macho hype and allow men other types of loving, acceptable behaviors. Strength and ruggedness are not bad qualities in themselves, but to use them to oppress others is unacceptable in any circumstance. Power needs to be equally shared by all responsible individuals--politically, economically, recreationally, and in the freedom to move about without fear for one's life. We pride ourselves on our country being the land of the free; however, we continue to promote and allow oppressive behavior to exist on a large scale as viewed nightly on our local news.

THE READER'S TURN:

1. The first task of the persuasive writer is to get the reader's attention. How does this writer dramatize the issue, and how effectively?
2. This writer does not mince words. Point out examples of strong language, and discuss their effect on the reader. Are there any striking phrases that you are going to remember? Strong language has been known to backfire. Does it here?
3. This writer writes from a sense of personal grievance. Where does it show most strongly? Does she succeed in making her readers see her own experience as part of a larger pattern? How or where?
4. Harsh negative criticism often implies a positive ideal by which offenders are judged. What positive ideal emerges from this paper, and how effectively?
5. This paper illustrates the kind of writing that makes a strong appeal to its readers. Prepare a reply showing how you respond to the author's plea.

Marriage: Bond or Bondage?

A huge percentage of people entering young adulthood today have come from broken families. Many of these young people who have been abandoned by mothers or fathers after watching countless fights and hostile, hateful divorces are not getting married; they're choosing to live together without the legal or traditionally spiritual bond of marriage. Recently, I had the opportunity to listen to some of these young people's views when a class of freshmen shared their ideas on marriage. All of these students' parents were either divorced, getting a divorce, or threatening to get a divorce, and all of these students looked at marriage as a kind of bondage, as the enemy of real love. They felt that divorce was or would be a liberating experience for their parents because it did or would free them to find new possibilities for satisfaction in their frustrated lives.

These young people and many like them see marriage as the greatest obstacle that love can meet. However, my grandparents have been married fifty-seven years, my parents have been married thirty-five years, I've been married twelve years, and from my experience and observation, I believe married life is synonymous with love life because the commitment and permanence marriage demands is what allows true, time-worn, battle-scarred, long-lived, proved, real love to develop. Most people enter marriage with achieving happiness in mind. They think the marriage will make them happy and make them feel good. When their happily-ever-after turns out to be filled with waves of depression, moments of fear and anxiety, or fits of anger, romantic lovers blame their partner and their marriage. They're sure something better is out there and that they're missing it. However, true love doesn't always feel good. I think true love is a thinking love, not just a feeling love. True lovers think of each other, so true love is hard work. Being selfish is a lot easier. Sitting for hours talking problems out and struggling to understand or be understood when you're dead tired from working an eight-hour day are part of love. Holding the head of someone who is throwing up, washing someone else's dirty socks, changing someone else's oil, and all those other dirty tasks are a part of love. Romantic infatuation is just love's conception. True love is born only through a period of gestation and labor pains. For a relationship to grow and work, both people have to be working hard. It's not easy. It just doesn't come. It takes time and the permanence of marriage allows that time.

 These young people would argue that love cannot be made permanent, and, certainly, marriage is not always permanent. Divorce of some sort has always existed and is acceptable and common now. These young people would argue that love should be free. However, free love isn't the same thing as bonded love. Free love stays only as long as it feels good. Free love is an easily separated love. I think for most people who are "happily" married, the definition of happiness is rather mild. I think people who have been married a considerable amount of time find a great deal of their satisfaction in their marriage from a deep feeling that here is something that won't suddenly go away, here is something solid and fundamentally unchanging in a changing world. This deep feeling and belief in the relationship can exist even when on the surface the impulse is to go away.

 I recently read an essay by a student on the trend of unmarried cohabitation. She said that if an unmarried couple "should find they aren't right together" they can separate on more friendly terms, knowing that they tried, they made a mistake, and they don't have to add public humiliation and legal red tape to their injured feelings. In reality, I don't think breaking off a relationship, if it's a serious relationship, is ever this easily done. Often, I think, the hassle of the legal red tape and the fear of public humiliation cause people to work out their problems. Without these hassles, people can easily run away from the relationship and their problems. These people usually find themselves in relationship after relationship on an endless quest for satisfaction. Within the bonds of marriage, people can learn to enjoy and maintain a relationship they've built. They can learn that being true to themselves and to their commitment to someone else, even when it doesn't feel good, feels good.

The young people I've listened to would argue that marriage is possession, and that no person should possess another. They seem to forget that people enter marriage pushed forward by loving feelings and a desire for companionship. Marriage becomes possession and bondage only when the people in it feel trapped and dissatisfied. A marriage should be a harmonized effort between two people to feel intimate, supportive, secure, and appreciated. Marriage becomes possession only when spouses take their partners for granted, smother them, and refuse to allow them to grow and change.

THE READER'S TURN:

1. Are the young people whose experiences and views are described in the first paragraph representative of young people as you know them? Are you one of them?

2. In the main part of her paper, the author systematically attacks misleading expectations. What is her strategy for changing the minds of readers who look for "romantic" love, who expect to be "happily married," or who look for "free love"?

3. The two concluding paragraphs try hard to make marriage sound good and to defuse possible objections. How does the author go about accomplishing these goals? How successful is she?

4. Much strong persuasive writing appeals to powerful basic feelings and needs that may not be fully spelled out. What basic feelings or needs does this paper bring into play? How widely do you think they are shared?

5. Prepare a paper in which you draw on your own experience and observation to give advice about love, courtship, marriage, divorce, dealing with parents, or a similar topic. How are you going to make your recommendations persuasive?

Justice

Three years ago I signed up to be a Big Sister to an eight-year-old girl through the Big Brothers/Big Sisters agency of the county. When the caseworker matched me with Sonia she warned me that Sonia's mother had decreed two topics as taboo for Sonia: sex and her father. I could somewhat understand the mother's prudery about sex, although I disagreed with it. But I was surprised and intrigued when the caseworker told me that Sonia's father was in a state prison, sentenced to death. I pitied the girl, wondering how she felt about having a father who brought her shame.

Sonia has rarely mentioned sex, so that part of the agreement was easy to keep. However, although I never brought up the subject of her father, I discussed how she felt about him whenever she wanted to discuss him. After about three months of seeing each other, Sonia told me that she had been to the movie _Pinocchio_ as a very little girl but she didn't remember it. She explained that she had fallen asleep in the car and her father had carried her into the theater, held her as she slept through the movie, and carried her out again. I was astonished that she had a warm memory of trusting a man who had raped and brutally killed two teenage girls. Then she said that she liked visiting him in jail because she and her brothers got to eat a lot at the prison. I didn't discourage her from talking; I was discovering that she loved her father and was not ashamed of him.

Not only does Sonia love her father, but she has the same need to idealize him as all children need to admire their parents. I remember being moved once when she startled me as we were driving downtown by pointing to a tall building and exclaiming, "There's my daddy's cell." I was confused, so I asked her to explain. She told me that he wasn't there at that time but he had spent some time in jail in the city and she remembered visiting him there. She had pointed with pride to a building she associated with her father, just as another child might say excitedly, "There's my daddy's office." I realized that her father, a vicious killer, was loved and needed. If capital punishment is reinstated in the state, she will lose her father and she will have to shift through an immense burden of conflicting feelings--grief, anger, shame, confusion. His death would help no one. His victims are already dead and his death can't bring them back. Perhaps their relatives want justice, but his death is not justice. It would simply be vengeance. By killing him, we can't bring back the innocent; we can only hurt more innocent people.

I have always been opposed to capital punishment. I believe that, as a society, our role is to care for and protect each other. When one of our members hurts others, we remove him or her from the rest. But killing that person as punishment seems to be sinking to a low level of ethics. Policies of vengeance and "an eye for an eye" morality serve only to escalate violence. We forbid people from killing each other, yet as a legal institution, society dictates that killing is acceptable only when it deems it necessary, as in times of war and as punishment for crimes. I believe that if, as a society, we refuse to accept violence among ourselves and refuse to punish the violent with death, we are carrying out a commitment to peace and non-violence.

Sonia has two pictures hanging in her bedroom that her father painted for her while imprisoned. One is of an Indian girl and the other of an eagle flying above a canyon. Sonia has told me that her father has painted a mural at the prison, as well. Perhaps she idealizes him in her ignorance; most people are guilty of idealizing imperfect people. Yet Sonia will be faced with the much harder job of reconciling her love for her father with the reality that he is a criminal. Most children only have to realize that their caretakers aren't strong, all-knowing, and perfect. To increase this child's pain for the sake of saving tax dollars or of satisfying the understandable, but impossible to achieve, needs for revenge that some people have, would be tragic. Allowing Sonia's father to live would save his family more pain, and it would allow our society to rise above ethics based on violence and revenge.

THE READER'S TURN:

1. The author leads us into the paper by sharing with us what she learns or discovers about the eight-year-old girl. What relationship does this approach set up between the author and the reader? How does it affect your view of the girl's father?
2. The writer does not reveal her opposition to capital punishment until halfway into the paper. What is the effect of or the strategy behind this delay? How does the effect differ from that of a head-on approach?
3. What effect does the mention of the paintings in the final paragraph have on the reader?
4. What is the core of the author's message? What are her basic convictions? To what standards does she appeal?
5. Describe an experience that brought you close to the human realities behind familiar abstractions, slogans, or statistics.

Go in Peace

Death has always been a dirty word--a word that most people try to sweep under the carpet. True, it is something very frightening, but it is also inevitable. It has been on my mind in recent months because of my aged grandmother's condition. Death has lingered near her as most of her close friends as well as all of her siblings have died. She told me one day that when it was her time she wanted to "go in peace." She said that she wanted no part of a hospital and tubes and machines. She wants to die and be done with it. Her words opened up new questions for me. What if there are tubes and machines and a long wait? How can she be spared prolonged agony?

Are we ever justified in shortening a person's suffering? The medical profession opposes mercy killing or euthanasia; it strictly adheres to the preservation of human life. But what do we consider the boundaries of life that is truly living? Should we not consider the dignity and the wishes of the person who is dying?

Doctors make their careers saving lives. All lives must come to an end at some point, but now the point of death is often postponed indefinitely as medical technology grows. A comatose person can be kept breathing for an indeterminate length of time, as was the case with Karen Quinlan. This young woman lived for years on life support until her family won a court battle to take her off the machinery that pumped her lungs full of air. Although her body remained alive for some time afterwards, she was never conscious. Many coma victims do die after being removed from the machines that allow them to function as they lie motionless in a hospital bed.

The medical profession does its job by keeping the person in a coma alive. That body with the tubes down the throat and the needles in the arm is a living thing. It is not the walking, talking person that loved ones have known, but its heart is beating and its lungs are rising thanks to medical technology. But what is the quality of that being's life? What has happened to its right of choice, which makes it a thinking creature?

Human beings notoriously fight for their rights--their rights to speech and liberty as well as their right to make decisions concerning their own bodies. Women can legally kill unborn babies through abortions with the help of the medical profession. They have control over the unborn, to decide for life or death. In the case of abortion, we deal with a life that is just beginning. In the case of a dying person, the medical person wants to keep the dying person alive, even if that person wants to die.

Suppose that a cancer patient feels that life is no longer worth living because of insufferable pain. What can the family do? The dying patient's pain is great, and the available choices are few. People should have the right to make choices concerning their own bodies. The patient has the right to die, enlisting the help of others if the patient chooses.

Suppose a person lies braindead. Is that still a full human being? Where is the dignity of such a patient? The family of the braindead person has the right to fight for the dignity of their loved one. If true living is no longer possible, they should be able to opt for death, not for a life in between.

My grandmother asked me what I will do when it comes time for her to die. I told her I would weep for her and be very sad, but I would remember how she lived. For me, this means that I could not let her linger in the life in between with machines and tubes. I must respect her wishes of how she wants to die. She must "go in peace" the way she plans, not the way a doctor plans. She chose the way she lived, and, with my help, she will choose the way she dies.

THE READER'S TURN:

1. How do the writer's introduction and conclusion humanize a very general problem? With what effect?
2. What picture does this paper present of the medical profession? Does the treatment of the medical profession seem sympathetic, biased, fair?
3. Which of the details or arguments in this paper are most telling or effective? Are you going to remember striking images or telling phrases?
4. Has this paper as a whole affected your thinking or changed your mind? Why or why not?
5. Have you ever felt that on an issue of current concern you hold a minority position or an unpopular view? Prepare a paper in which you try to make the majority understand your point of view.

WRITING TOPICS 7

The best logical argument will not advance our cause if we cannot get people to care. Frightened or angry people are not likely to listen to reason if we are unable to reassure them or calm them down. To persuade reluctant readers, we have to reckon with their interests, feelings, and loyalties. Effective persuasion often combines logical argument with a frank appeal to the reader's emotions and values. (Propaganda and the hard sell often dispense with logic altogether, playing on the reader's emotions and prejudices instead.)

1. The Bottom Line: Fund raisers, like people who make commercials, are judged by results. Draft a fund-raising letter designed to raise money for a cause you support. Have your classmates serve as your trial audience. Have them explain why they would or would not respond to your appeal.
2. An Urgent Plea: Getting people to vote for lower taxes is easy. Our powers of persuasion are put to the test when we ask people to give up something to which they have become used or addicted. Write an urgent plea designed to make your contemporaries give up smoking, drinking, unsafe sex, recreational drugs, spitting in public, or other undesirable habits. Give some serious thought to what might work and what is likely to be tuned out.

3. **Fighting Neglect:** Many voters are cynical about the chances of alerting local officials to instances of neglect or to abuses. Can you think of an outstanding example of neglect or abuse that would make you want to try anyway? Write a letter designed to get the attention of officials who might be in a position to remedy the situation.

4. **Arousing Public Opinion:** Do you ever feel moved to outrage or indignation? Write a letter-to-the-editor designed to make an apathetic public share your concern. Give serious thought to your overall strategy.

5. **A Self-Advertisement:** Do you ever feel misunderstood or unloved? Write a "To-Whom-It-May-Concern" letter that will help others (classmates, alienated former friends, prospective friends) appreciate your good qualities.

Part Three

Writing Across the Curriculum

Students sometimes come to feel that writing matters mostly in English classes. In actual fact, of course, writing is the central medium of communication in many areas across the curriculum. People in many fields write in order to circulate information, conduct arguments over conflicting theories and approaches, and share their knowledge with a larger audience.

The student writers in the third part of this collection do not write about special fields of interest as specialists writing for specialists. Instead, in several areas of specialized interest, they write about topics that concern, or should concern, the general public.

How much of what scientists, media critics, or historians care about can they communicate to the public at large? The first group of papers illustrates the kind of science writing that faces the issues raised by progress in science and technology. The second group illustrates the kind of media criticism that looks with serious attention and often with alarm at the way the media shape our view of the world. The third looks at social issues that are too urgent to remain the private province of social scientists. The fourth and final group looks at imaginative literature from the point of view of the common reader.

8
Science Writing:
The Uses and Abuses of Science

Much writing in the modern world is designed to share the findings of science, to celebrate its promise, and to warn against its side effects. Much science writing is motivated by the need to help knowledge catch up with ignorance: To understand scientific findings we need to take in the results of close observation, pay attention to technical detail, and do some coherent thinking. The great popularizers like Isaac Asimov or Carl Sagan have the knack of making difficult scientific information intelligible and accessible for large numbers of educated readers.

What makes science writing provocative is that science is not just a convenient practical tool for building faster computers or ovens that cook our food in an instant. When put to work in the service of modern medicine, science becomes a matter of health and sickness, life and death. When dealing with such questions as whether the sun is in orbit around the earth or whether we are biological cousins of the chimpanzee, scientists have drastically shaken up traditional religious views and values. Today, we hear numerous voices warning us that scientific progress has gone too far, giving us a world that it polluted and booby-trapped with nuclear weapons, tempting us to play God as we splice genes and produce test-tube babies.

How well do the student writers in this group accomplish the twin goals of much good science writing: to shed light on a scientific subject, and to alert us to its larger implications?

Was Granddad a Monkey?

Four hundred years after the Copernican revolution, there is still a Flat Earth Society. Will it take a similar span of time before we come to terms with Darwin's theories about our relation to the animal kingdom?

Ice-Minus: The Chilling Effect

In a world threatened by mass famine, genetic engineering making plants more resistant to frost or disease holds out great promise. Yet our fears about releasing mutant new species into the environment have a chilling effect.

Fighting the "I Feel Fat" Diseases in the Schools

For the person battling a cruel debilitating disease, better understanding and scientific progress are often the last best hope.

Whose Children Are These?

A person is not an incubator: Surrogate mothers are human beings entitled to legal protection, moral scruples, and second thoughts. This paper encourages us to have some serious second thoughts about the legality of surrogate motherhood.

Was Granddad a Monkey?

Evolution--the theory and the word--has been the center of controversy from the time the theory was established in the nineteenth century until today.

Most scientists are quick to point out that evolution means a "change through time." Evolution is a natural, gradual change in a species, not an individual member of a species, through a long period of time.

Most uninformed people, when confronted with the word evolution think of Darwin and the misconceptions surrounding his theory. They believe that Darwin thought that man, as he is today, had primates, and particularly apes as we see them today, as direct ancestors. Of course this is an absurd notion.

Charles Darwin was the staff naturalist aboard the HMS Beagle, a British survey and mapping vessel. In the course of his observations in South America and on the Galapagos Islands, he noted that geographically separated species were similar enough to be related but exhibited differences unique to each particular location. Based upon many observations, years of further research and years of pondering what he had seen, he established his theory of Natural Selection. The idea of evolution was not new when Darwin wrote "The Origin of Species," but his restatement, with the added punch of Natural Selection, rocked the world.

Modern science has revealed the mechanism that drives natural selection. Within the genetic code which determines our physical makeup, random changes or mutations occur quite naturally and frequently. Usually these mutations make no difference positive or negative for the individual possessing them. However, occasionally a mutation may give the individual some advantage in its environment. That is the key.

An example of an advantage might be a slightly longer neck for a giraffe, enabling that individual to reach the tender juicy leaves out of reach of other giraffes. This individual would have a better chance to survive and reproduce and pass on the genetic mutation. The longer neck is thus "selected for" in this environment. An unusually short neck would similarly be "selected against," as the individual possessing that trait would be unlikely to survive to reproduce. The theory states that individuals could not arbitrarily grow a longer neck, but the longer-necked offspring should survive to reproduce. On the other hand, the short-necked genes in the population would die out through competition for food. Thus, with enough time, the giraffe population would all have the advantageous longer neck.

Darwin stated that through this process, natural selection, a species could and would change through time, evolving to adapt to its environment. Contrary to popular misconception, Darwin did not say that an individual from the population could change to suit environmental changes.

This country is currently divided into two distinct camps on this subject, the "Evolutionists" and the "Creationists." Creationists believe the world was created by God in six days. They further believe man to be a separate and distinct creation, not part of nature, and certainly not the current step in a long chain of minute changes. Evolutionists, on the other hand, believe in a world billions of years old, and that species, including man, evolved over millions of years.

Laws have been and continue to be passed on both sides of the issue. Tennessee still has the Butler Act on the books. Texas for a time banned texts that teach evolution. On the other hand, it was against the law to hint at a Divine hand in creation in California schools. Unfortunately, the evolutionists and the creationists both loudly thump their books and tightly close their minds.

Having been raised in a Christian home, science classes were a problem for me at first. Having put a great deal of thought, and prayer, into the issue, I've come up with a model which works for me. In Genesis, God said He created the world and all that lives on it. He did not say how. The only clue He offers is that time doesn't work for Him as it does for us. This fits well into modern science's picture of change over eons of time.

Darwin never left God out of the picture. How could he? He devoutly believed in God. Most scientists will admit that Something powers the universe--and that includes the random changes which may or may not be transmitted to the next generation. This hybrid approach to two seemingly antithetic issues is supported by a growing number of people who call themselves Scientific Creationists.

Species do change. Whether or not you believe in God, you must recognize that fossil records indicate changes. Even humans have caused some species to evolve. All of our domestic animals were selectively bred from wild species. We forced evolution by selecting for characteristics we wanted.

In Nature, evolution is a natural, gradual change in a species, not an individual, over a long period of time. Darwinism does not exclude Divine Creation. Narrow-(or closed-)mindedness causes problems, not the theories. Controversy will probably continue until our species evolves into something more reasonable.

THE READER'S TURN:

1. Basic requirements for successful science writing include clear definition of key terms, clear explanation of basic processes, and strategic use of instructive examples. Does this paper meet these requirements? How or where?

2. Part of a science writer's job often is to clear up misunderstandings or misconceptions. Where or how does this writer do so?

3. Some of the best science writing is not dryly impersonal but reflects a strong personal interest or commitment. What is the "personal connection" in this paper?

4. What has been your own exposure to the controversies swirling around evolution? Have you heard of the Monkey Trial? What stand would you take on the issue?

5. Major theories from the Copernican hypothesis to Freud's theory of repression or Marx's theory of surplus value have shaped the thinking of people in the modern world. Write a paper about one major theory in the natural or social sciences that has been an eye-opener for you.

Ice-Minus: The Chilling Effect

In a small strawberry patch in Castroville, on a quarter-acre potato field in Tulelake, a historic experiment--the first release of genetically altered bacteria onto an open field--was to have taken place. These two small farming communities in Northern California resolutely stood their ground and refused to allow scientists to use their lands for the experiments. If the experiment was successful, the new bacteria could save farmers hundreds of millions of dollars by protecting crops from frost damage. If the worst fears were realized, the bacteria could literally stop the rain. The biotechnology industry has promised spectacular achievements in agriculture; this first experiment was merely a small step towards the goal of ending world hunger. But the substantial benefits the farmers may receive may be outweighed by the risks of environmental damage as yet unknown. The people in these two rural communities measured the risks and said no to the promises of science.

The controversy began in 1983 when Steven Lindlow, a plant pathologist at the University of California at Berkeley, applied to the National Institute of Health (NIH) to test genetically altered bacteria at the University's research site in Tulelake near the Oregon border. The NIH approved the test, but an environmental group, Foundation for Economic Trends, headed by Jeremy Rifkin, succeeded in delaying the tests through a court action stating that the NIH did not have sufficient tests to prove what long-range effects the altered bacteria might have on the environment. In November, 1985, a biotechnical company, Advanced Genetic Sciences (AGS), received approval from the Environmental Protection Agency (EPA) for basically the same experiment to be tested on land near Castroville in Monterey County. In 1986, the Monterey County Board of Supervisors enacted an emergency land-use ordinance aimed at stopping the experiments in Castroville. Zoning laws were rewritten to outlaw the tests in the county at the request of alarmed citizens and environmental groups.

The object of all the controversy is the microscopic <u>Pseudomonas Syringae</u>, common bacteria found on most plants. The bacteria cause frost damage and ruin many crops each year, not because the frost chills the plants, but because crystals form in plant tissues and wound them. Lindlow was among the first researchers to modify the bacteria by eliminating the protein, found on the surface of the bacteria, that causes ice crystals to form when the temperature dips below freezing. He did this by identifying the gene responsible for the ice-nucleating protein, removing it, splicing back into the bacteria a gene from other bacteria that don't have the ice-forming trait, and then cloning the altered bacteria. The altered bacteria can then be sprayed on crops. The researchers hope that the altered "ice-minus" bacteria will colonize a plant in the early blossom stage of development when frost is most threatening. They simply want it to live long enough, about two to six weeks, to ward off the naturally occurring "ice-positive" bacteria during this dangerous period. "As the plant grows, there will be opportunities for the wild [natural] type [of bacteria] to come in," said Douglas Sarojak, AGS's Director of Marketing. "What we hope is that the blossom will develop into a sufficiently mature fruit that is no longer sensitive to frost." In the greenhouse, the bacteria have survived long enough to do that, but in an open field, where they will be subjected to changing weather patterns or competition from other organisms, researchers don't know for sure how well they will do.

The fears of the public and other scientists are based on just that uncertainty. One fear is that the "ice-minus" bacteria will bully their way onto nearby plants and crowd out their unaltered cousins. Researchers admit that the bacteria will spread beyond the test plot, but expect they will dissipate in such small numbers as to make them barely detectable. Also, the mutant bacteria not containing the protein exist in nature and have not asserted themselves and dominated the ice-positive strain. But opponents warn that the gene-spliced strain was engineered by humans, and it might exhibit properties that are undesirable. Rifkin insists that more tests are needed to determine if the bacteria will harm other plants, whether they pose any health risks to residents in the vicinity, and whether the organism will die out, as its proponents contend it will, or reproduce at uncontrollable rates, as he fears it might. Rifkin calls the bacteria "exotic" and likens them to organisms imported to this country from other parts of the world such as Dutch elm disease and the gypsy moth, which, he says, "went berserk and caused all kinds of havoc."

Even if the spreading of the bacteria does not occur, the spraying of thousands of acres of crops has other hazards. Some scientists now believe the protein plays an important role in the formation of ice crystals that evolve into snowflakes and raindrops. Russell C. Snell, an atmospheric researcher with the Cooperative Institute for Research in Environmental Studies at the University of Colorado, who was one of the discoverers of the ice-nucleating protein, is convinced that the loss of the ice-positive bacteria would cause droughts. Evidence for his arguments, he says, is that rainfall ceased in some areas of South America when jungles were cut down.

Many atmospheric scientists sharply disagree with Snell. The idea that gene-spliced bacteria pose a threat is "ridiculous," says Vincent Schaeffer, Director Emeritus of the Atmospheric Science and Research Center at the State University of New York at Albany. He argues that most rains begin in the high atmosphere, where temperatures are so cold that nucleating particles do not play a role.

But Snell is not easily brushed off. His theory is "not tested, but it's important enough that it should be tested," says Bagor Vali, head of the Atmospheric Science Department of the University of Wyoming. Jack Koyle, who heads an agricultural project for the nonprofit Environmental Policy Institute in Washington, D.C., agrees. Although a small field test might not cause harm, Doyle wonders, "what happens when you put this on 45,000 acres of potatoes?"

The doubts that the researchers are ready to test in open fields have caused delays for over three years. For the biotechnical companies, the delays and increased expenses for further testing could mean disaster. Arthur Kelman, a plant pathologist at the University of Wisconsin, says, "A lot of companies will go under because they can't test their products. The leadership of the United States in this area of science will be lost if we continue to let the lunatic fringe and some well-meaning honest people delay what logically has to happen next." Lindlow adds that the test should proceed since over fifty scientists have reviewed the experiment at the EPA and declared it safe.

But environmentalists and ecologists argue that the government lacks the ability to predict the environmental effects of releasing organisms outside contained laboratories. "I don't think we have a science base that allows us to make reasonable, sound predictions about what might happen," says Doyle. "The EPA has done as good a job as they can do, but there are enormous holes in its evaluation."

Farmers at Tulelake are concerned over the scientists' inability to agree and the questions left unanswered. They're unsure that the experiment is in their best interest. In 1986, 450 Tulelake residents continued their fight to delay the experiment by signing a petition calling for a halt until health and safety questions are answered. Farmers say they can't afford the notoriety that might follow the historic experiment. "Who knows in which way our competition might use this information to discredit our product? If something goes wrong and we get a blackball in our area, boy, will it cost us," said Lowell Kenyon who farms 1,000 acres of potatoes. The farmers in the area believe the fear of bacteria could torpedo the market for potatoes just like the discovery of pesticide contamination wiped out the market for California watermelons in 1985.

In the interest of business and the furtherance of an important discovery in science, testing needs to be done on open fields. But the question of how the organisms will react outside the laboratory on the environment cannot yet be measured. Until these uncertainties can be ascertained, research should be contained in the laboratory. "We're putting something into the environment and we have no idea what its response is going to be to the ecosystem around it," said Andrew Kimbrell, an attorney who is policy director for the Foundation on Economic Trends. "That is just irresponsible." And for the farmer, if the nightmares of some scientists come true, they may wish they had never heard of "ice-minus."

THE READER'S TURN:

1. Who is the intended audience for this paper? Do you think this paper effectively reaches the intended audience?

2. How does the first paragraph of this paper bring the issue into focus? What are key questions that the writer wants us to ponder? What examples dramatize these questions most effectively?

3. What technical information or scientific concepts do we need to grasp to follow the writer's argument? How well does the paper communicate technical information?
4. Does this writer give a fair hearing to both sides of the controversy? How would you sum up the two conflicting positions?
5. What decision would *you* make on this issue? What reasons would you give to justify your decision? Would you need more information? What kind?

Fighting the "I Feel Fat" Diseases in the Schools

Many female students in today's junior high schools, high schools, and colleges are suffering from two diseases which may be prevented by establishing programs that inform students and teachers about the diseases. Anorexia nervosa and bulimia are two severe eating disorders afflicting increasing numbers of adolescent girls and young women. By educating teachers, students, and even parents if possible of the causes and devastating effects of these illnesses, many of the girls who are at risk for developing an eating disorder may be spared and those already afflicted may be directed towards sources of help.

Both anorexia nervosa and bulimia are psychological illnesses that have tremendous physical manifestations. Although occasionally boys or men develop one of these eating disorders, most of those who have anorexia nervosa and bulimia are female. A girl who is anorexic is starving herself. Typically, she has recently reached puberty and she has become emaciated by dieting to lose weight. She may have lost over 25% of her original weight, but she does not see herself as too thin. In fact, she has become so obsessed with food and is so terrified of becoming fat that she continues to diet. Bulimics, like anorexics, are characterized by what the late Dr. Hilde Bruch, a professor of psychiatry at Baylor College of Medicine, called "the relentless pursuit of thinness." Bulimics, however, cannot fast indefinitely; instead they are trapped in a vicious cycle of "binge eating" and "purging." In other words, they eat enormous quantities of food and then make themselves vomit or take laxatives. Sometimes anorexics will binge eat but fast and exercise frantically rather than purge after binge eating.

As a recovered anorexic and bulimic, I am very concerned by what I have read of the increase of these eating disorders. I have a "sixth sense" for detecting bulimics, just as some recovered alcoholics can spot fellow addicts. I first discovered a fellow bulimic when I returned after six months away from home. When my 15-year-old sister greeted me at the airport weighing at least 30 pounds less than she had when I left and looking very thin, I worried. When my mother told me she ate cream of mushroom soup cold out of the can and sometimes canned hams and roasts disappeared from the refrigerator, I suspected she was bulimic. When I asked my sister why there was a spoon on the tank of the toilet in her bathroom, she confirmed my fear, telling me she used the handle to scrape the back of her throat in order to make herself gag. I was overcome with rage, blaming my mother for both of our eating sicknesses. I know now that families can contribute to the development of anorexia and bulimia, but cultural pressures are also major factors.

I believe that many women who have suffered and currently suffer from eating disorders might have been helped if taught in school about the dangers of dieting, both psychological and physiological. When a group of my friends and I became anorexic, we whispered among ourselves about dieting and about the girl who dropped out of school to be hospitalized. No teacher tried to intervene. Most of us fought battles at home with our parents about eating; at school we competed with each other to lose more weight. Bulimics, who often don't lose much weight, can disguise their illness for years from family and friends. Schools cannot treat eating disorders any more than they can treat alcoholism, drug abuse, or AIDS. Schools can, nevertheless, arm students with knowledge that they can use to help themselves and each other prevent and combat harmful dieting obsessions.

Most anorexics are adolescent girls and young women from educated and middle class or upper class homes. Before becoming anorexic, these females tend to be perfectionists, very critical of themselves, and obsessional. They often see life in all-or-none, rigid terms. They set goals for themselves which are virtually unobtainable, and then work very hard to achieve those goals. They also tend to be introverted and overly compliant, wanting desperately to please and be accepted. As they lose weight, some of these traits become even more pronounced.

Inside, anorexics feel distressed and helpless to control their feelings; controlling their weight gives them a feeling of effectiveness which they become desperately afraid to give up. They become so obsessed with starving themselves that they lose the ability to recognize their hunger and to see their body accurately. Bruch wrote "These patients suffer from an overriding, all-pervasive sense of ineffectiveness, of not being in control of their body and its functions, of mistrusting as pretense or fraud any thoughts or feelings originating within themselves." They believe that by becoming thin, a point which they continue to associate with lower and lower weights, their problems will be solved and they will feel good about themselves at last.

Most bulimics are also perfectionists; most have rigid, either-or thinking; and most have low self-esteem. Bulimics rely on the opinions of others to evaluate their worth. They want to appear attractive to others and value self-control.

Dieting precedes the development of both anorexia nervosa and bulimia in nearly every case. Anorexics cement their rigid self-control and fast; bulimics give in to their hunger, and believing in all-or-nothing dieting, binge eat after they have lost control. Why do so many teenage girls diet? Some researchers point to society's pressure on women to be thin. Dr. Arnold E. Anderson, a professor of psychiatry at The Johns Hopkins University School of Medicine, wrote that anorexia nervosa "occurs only in societies that value thinness despite abundant food." Dr. Paul E. Garfinkel and Dr. Allan S. Kaplan, psychiatrists at Toronto General Hospital, wrote that some researchers "argued that the pressures on women to meet the current thinner standard for physical attractiveness are responsible for the preoccupation with dieting. The fashion industry and media have encouraged the association between thinness and success, beauty, wealth, and happiness."

All girls, and especially girls who are psychologically vulnerable to eating disorders, need support in combatting society's pressure to lose weight. Programs designed to prevent the development of eating disorders are desperately needed in schools. Educational programs should offer information about nutrition and the physiological and psychological consequences of prolonged dieting. They should emphasize that our culture determines standards of thinness that are biologically unattainable for many women unless they starve themselves. The programs should also point out that girls are often still socialized to be passive and dependent, qualities which conflict with the more modern requirements for women to become independent and competent in careers. Prevention programs should allow girls to discuss among themselves their ideas of what it means to be "feminine" and what choices and goals they have for their futures. Since so many girls are unhappy with their bodies and diet to lose weight, prevention programs ought to help girls learn to accept their bodies and reject cultural prototypes.

THE READER'S TURN:

1. The definitions of the two disorders described in the second paragraph are models of how to translate abstruse technical information into clear everyday language. Point out and discuss examples of plain English in the paragraph.

2. This paper draws on a mix of personal first-hand experience and authoritative sources. Where does the "personal connection" first become clear? (Why do you think the writer did not spell it out in the first paragraph?)

3. Trace the author's analysis of the psychological and social causes of the disorders. Do you find the analysis convincing? Do all or parts of it surprise you?

4. What is the range of expert opinion that the author draws on? What use does she make of it?

5. Millions of people in our society seem to suffer from afflictions for which modern medicine does not (or not yet) have an answer. Investigate one of these to see if there is any hope for the future.

Whose Children Are These?

"I can not remember if the day was sunny or dreary . . . . I lost my sense of awareness during the twenty-six hour labor before my son was born that Sunday morning, November 9, 1980. My newborn son lay peacefully in the arms of his new mother: not in my arms." These are the words of Elizabeth Kane, the nation's first legal surrogate mother, eight years after delivering the son she has never seen since.

Like many surrogate mothers she thought it would not matter to her if she ever saw her child again. She had vowed not to intrude on the lives of her son, his biological father, and his new mother. "Eight months after the birth of my son, I was still unable to push away the thought of him," said Ms. Kane in a recent interview. What she imagined as a selfless act for an unknown family turned out to be a selfish act toward her own family. "What right did I have to put them through a test of courage I thought would be only mine to bear? I had no idea my children would bond with their brother during the pregnancy or would spend years to come aching for the touch or sound of him." Like many so-called surrogate mothers Ms. Kane now believes that what she did is not right. She has never tried to see or get her son back as she feels it would cause too much damage, but on Mother's Day she aches for that child and realizes that she is not a surrogate mother but a birth mother. She also realizes she will never be able to get over having given him away.

Many women say that their participation in "surrogate" parenting had begun with a deep empathy for childless couples. They feel every infertile couple has a right to a child genetically linked to at least one parent. Most legal surrogate mothers are married and already have children. They feel that they are helping others and doing them a great favor. The money couldn't be much of a factor as legal surrogate mothers are paid between $8,000 to $20,000. Ask any woman walking down the street if she would take that amount of money for carrying a child for nine months and then give that child up at birth: The answer would be no! At least that's the response I got when I asked five different women on campus.

The recent trail regarding Baby M received nationwide coverage. Following giving birth to Baby M, her surrogate mother (birth mother) Mary Beth Whitehead decided that she did not want to give her child up and wanted legal custody. After a long-drawn-out battle Judge Sorkow of New Jersey awarded custody of Melissa to her biological father, William Stern. The case was promptly appealed to New Jersey's Supreme Court. Even if Judge Sorkow were upheld on every point, the defenders of surrogate motherhood and the entrepreneurs who profit from its promotion may find that the case has not been entirely to their advantage. It has even persuaded some observers whose ethics are strictly pragmatic that the bad effects of surrogacy outweigh the good.

Surrogate parenting is wrong. I shudder to think of the loss of self-esteem when today's surrogate children are told they were bought and sold. I can only imagine what will take place years from now when these children are grown and hire attorneys. Will they sue their fathers for denying them the right to have relationships with their biological mothers? Will they sue their birth mothers for signing them away before they were even conceived? Is this a better fate for these children than having never being born? What right do we have to play God? Is it necessary to do something just because we have the technology?

What rights do the children have? In Florida a woman was contracted to carry a child for a couple. On delivery she would be paid $10,000 for a girl child and $15,000 for a boy child; she delivered twins, one of each. The biological father and new mother were only legally responsible to take one child and they wanted the boy. What rights do these children have? The birth mother said she would keep and raise both rather than have the children split up, but the biological father is fighting for custody of the boy.

The questions surrogacy raises are deeply disturbing. Do we have the right to make children for those who can't? Just because the technology is available is it morally and ethically sound for a woman to carry a child that she will never see again after birth? What price do we put on our children's life? A surrogate mother is a substitute for a natural parent, but isn't the birth parent the natural parent? The idea of surrogacy and the issues around it need to be thought over in greater detail and long and hard before any more children are dragged through the courts or separated from their twins or for that matter their natural siblings.

THE READER'S TURN:

1. Who is the intended audience for this paper?

2. What are the key issues that the writer wants the readers to ponder? What examples dramatize these issues most effectively?

3. This paper never makes a mystery of the author's sympathies or opinions. What are some of the ways these become clear? Does the paper try to be fair to the other side?

4. Who is to blame? Where and how does the paper point the finger? Do you think the accusations are justified?

5. Where do you stand on the issues raised in this paper? Do you think the developments examined in this paper are part of a larger trend? What are other related developments or further examples?

WRITING TOPICS 8

A vast amount of writing is published each year to explain to us the findings of science, to keep us informed of its applications, to warn us of its dangers, and to chart for us its probable future course. In innumerable ways, science and the technology it has created have changed the way we live and the way we look at the world. Try your hand at writing papers that will leave your readers better informed about scientific or technical subjects.

1. **Keeping Informed:** Help newspaper readers understand a scientific concept currently in the news. What is desertification—how does it work? What is the greenhouse effect? What is the ozone layer, and what is happening to it? What do we need to know about the earth's crust in order to understand earthquakes? Make a special effort to explain technical terms and processes.

2. **The Cutting Edge:** Much science writing tries to satisfy our curiosity about the latest breakthroughs or about developments on the cutting edge of research. Bring your readers up to date on a topic like laser applications, atomic fusion, alternatives to heart surgery, superconductivity, or new approaches to treating mental illness. Help your readers see the significance of new developments.

3. **Side Effects:** In recent years, much science writing has sounded dire warnings about the harmful side effects of technological progress. Are we losing the battle against air pollution? How are we dealing with radioactive wastes? Are pesticides contaminating our food supply? Are we losing the

battle to clean up our rivers? Research one such topic and prepare a factual, balanced status report for the concerned reader.

4. Science Fact and Fiction: Some of the best science fiction project current trends into the future. It makes us say: "That's exactly how it's going to be!" Describe the future as projected in a favorite work of science fiction and show it to be the logical end result of current trends.

5. The World View of Science: Modern science has often posed a challenge to traditional ideas and values. Is creationism compatible with modern scientific knowledge? Can a religious person accept the theory of evolution? Are scientists who create test-tube babies or develop gene splicing playing God? Can science help us define when human life begins or when it legally ends? Research and discuss one serious ethical or philosophical question raised by modern developments in science.

9
Media Watch: The Critical Viewer

We often think of television and movies as strictly entertainment—an escape from reality into a harmless fantasy world. But at the same time we realize that the images we see on the screen help shape our view of the world in which we live. Obviously, programs and movies cater to prejudices or challenge them; they create or counteract stereotypes; they make us more sensitive to urgent social needs (or make us more callous and hard-boiled about them).

When we look at the entertainment media critically, we assume that they have the power to reinforce or challenge established ways of thinking; they have the potential for narrowing or widening our horizons. Even people who clamor for censorship of what they consider offensive or subversive pay the media the compliment of taking them seriously.

Look at what the student critics in this group found worth thinking and writing about in what they saw on the screen:

Soap Opera: The Modern Tragedy

This journal entry is looking for what has remained constant in popular spectacles—whether presented in an outdoor theater in ancient Greece or piped into our living rooms via the tube.

Cashing In: A Television Perspective of Business

A large part of the load the mail carrier totes to network headquarters consists of letters from viewers who were offended by how their group (women, Italians, pitbull fanciers) was pictured on the screen. This writer views with alarm the way popular television programs portray American business.

Realism and Ratings

This student editorial voices a frequently heard charge: The media pounce on a hot current issue in order to sensationalize and exploit it rather than in order to educate the populace.

The Last Temptation

Every so often, a book, a movie, or a television program brings out the would-be censors in force. In this paper, a graduate student and accomplished creative writer explores the mentality of the censor.

Soap Opera: The Modern Tragedy

When reading through the ancient Greek tragedies, I can't help but notice parallels between these exciting dramas and today's often popular soap operas. Certainly I do not mean to compare the quality of today's soap operas to the fine qualities elicited in the ancient dramas but rather to compare their nature or reasons for which both the ancient and modern stories have survived. I believe the basic parallel between the ancient Greek dramas and today's soap operas is the human fascination with emotional conflict and trauma.

The perfect set-up for a traumatic emotional conflict can be found within interpersonal relationships. We know the ancient Greeks often examined and scrutinized the personal intertwining of characters. The ancient play Oedipus Rex is one of the best examples of a complex entanglement of characters. The entire basis of the modern soap opera lies within the twisted entanglement of its characters. If all the modern characters were able to control, if not halt, their sexual promiscuity, there would be no more story lines.

There are other parallels to be drawn from the ancient drama and the modern soap opera, such as the use of ongoing plots and familiar characters. The Greek theatergoer already knew the story he was going to see. The dramas were based on well known legends and myths, and often characters from one play would be seen again in another (i.e., Creon who was in both Oedipus Rex and Antigone), in which the character's story was continued. Our modern soap operas are similar in that they too employ ongoing plots and familiar characters. The modern viewer generally knows what to expect from each character, because the characters are seen on a daily basis. We recognize the villain, the naive, and the sultry vixens through their actions in the everyday story.

In ancient times the prior knowledge of the dramas helped to build dramatic irony, that is to say, the audience became more excited because they knew what was going to happen while the characters on stage didn't, and the anticipation of the inevitable action became very stimulating for the audience. The familiarity of today's characters also adds a similar dramatic irony for the modern viewer. Even though today's viewer may not know precisely what the actual situational endings will be, the viewer has a fairly good idea about how each character will behave because by the nature of the soap opera: The "good" guys stay "good" and the "bad" guys stay "bad"; their behaviors are predictable.

Another similarity between the Greek drama and modern soap opera is the lack of emphasis on violence. In ancient times no violence took place on stage; we only heard about it through messengers. Today's soap operas have very few violent acts committed on screen, and even if so, these acts are not descriptively grisly.

We as humans have an innate curiosity about the relationships of others. Our social relationships have been explored by the early Greeks, and are still under examination in our society today. And I will venture to guess that as long as there are people, the impetus for the tragic human drama, on whatever level, will remain.

THE READER'S TURN:

1. Many critics keep highbrow art and lowbrow entertainment strictly separate, making sure that never the twain shall meet. Do you think this writer had a point in juxtaposing these two very different genres?

2. Which of the points of comparison do you find most convincing or instructive, which least?

3. Can you help this writer find concrete examples to flesh out the overview given in this journal entry? Sketch out supporting evidence the writer might want to use.

4. Can you give a striking example of what makes a serious play you have seen or read *different* from soap opera?

5. Some critics have taken the great classics of popular entertainment—from *Gone with the Wind* and *Star Trek* to *Star Wars* and *Rambo*—seriously for what they reveal about our values or our self-image as a nation. Take a serious look at a great popular classic from this point of view.

Cashing In: A Television Perspective of Business

A young man stands rigidly, a telephone receiver in one hand and a canister of frozen bull semen in the other. He is nervously fielding offers from two competing parties, a U.S. government agent and a Cuban national, for the procreative matter that he has stolen from an American: It is an adequate quantity to create a herd of miniaturized cattle, enough to feed the hungry masses on the chaff left from the wheat harvest. Both threaten him concerning the high price he demands. His answer: "Hey, I'm a capitalist!" Neither of the bidders contradicts him.

The above scene occurred on an episode of *Miami Vice*, but it is symptomatic of an entire genre of television shows that portray business people of all levels of economic success as thieves. A single week's viewing provides plenty of negative and rapacious business figures but few and only marginally responsible role models. The television model for success does not include people in private business, unless they are "working for the poor." Hence on *L.A. Law*, a lawyer takes a case for free to pull down "that awful big business" for the sake of some impoverished woman who lit her son's flame retardant pyjamas on fire and wants damages from the manufacturer of the pyjamas. To ask this woman for compensation as an attorney is immoral in T.V. land. To sue someone even when the plaintiff is grossly negligent or, in this case, grossly responsible for the disaster is moral.

In comedy, the business person, particularly the supervisor or "boss," is either a clown or an incompetent tyrant in search of a whipping boy on whom to blame failure. On *9 to 5*, the boss is a "300-pound pitbull with a necktie" who says, "I lie, I lie a lot, I like lies, and I feel good about that." On *Taxi*, the boss offers to show a female employee the Sistine Chapel as Michaelangelo saw it, i.e. on her back, and calls all of his subordinates "losers." The few examples of good professional people, like the Huxtables of *The Cosby Show*, are rarely seen working and some mention of charity is always made when the topic of the shows concerns money. The greatest "advocate of business" seen on T.V. was *Family Ties*' Alex P. Keaton, a college student who worshipped Nixon and money and who was supposed to represent the business mind. Here is the crux of a growing problem.

The evening soap operas are built around the struggle of a group of unscrupulous rich folk out to gain control of a business by any means, legal or otherwise. The characters of *Dallas* spent season upon season fighting over the chairmanship of Ewing Oil while trying to edge out their competitor, Cliff Barnes. J.R. Ewing became almost a synonym for dirty business dealings.

In light of all of this, one may ask why business continues to sponsor programs that question its reputation. I called a Bank of America public relations representative who agreed to speak to me candidly if I did not use her name. She told me that the primary goal of all advertising is to "get the product name out there so that people know you're here," but the secondary goal was simply to present the business in a positive light to counteract the message of the programs.

A recent spate of Chevron ads fit this example. In them kit foxes are protected from their natural predators, production in oilfields is stopped for the sake of mating birds, and sandblasted industrial equipment is placed in the ocean to create feeding habitats for fish. Weyerhauser ads have featured baby fawns protected in company forests. Both of these ads were prompted by claims that business is unecological; neither shows the real advantages that these industries bring in terms of providing housing, movement of foodstuffs, or transportation for humans.

When queried whether this wasn't buying equal time, she responded affirmatively, adding, "The people at the networks are funny. If they believe their shows, then they think we got our money by killing people." She then cited a show in which an investment banker killed a competitor who was successfully luring away clientele with a better package, though she has never heard an actual incident of this kind.

She continued by saying, "But they still want our money. You notice they never talk about money on the shows. You hear the word 'crap' used in a more polite way than 'money,' but just let you be late with ad payments and hear them howl."

I ended the interview by asking if the prognosis for change was good. "No," she said. "The power brokers aren't going to let go. They think we're bad because we want money. Nobody thinks about what they want, and that's power over other people's lives: what they see, think, hear . . . . They want to keep things their way."

We would not allow a racial, ethnic, religious, or sex group to be treated in this way. Why, then, should we allow people's choice of a legitimate profession to prejudice the way we view them?

THE READER'S TURN:

1. What is this writer's central complaint, and how does the introduction lead up to it?
2. Early in the paper, this writer lays down a barrage of examples from personal viewing. Do they seem representative or fair? Do any of them impress you especially or make you think?
3. According to this paper, what is the nature of the corporate image-building that is designed to counteract negative stereotypes about business? What is the writer's objection to it?
4. The concluding paragraphs of this paper mount an attack on the ethics and credibility of the networks. What is the charge?
5. Is this writer being oversensitive? Are people who speak up for other groups that feel misrepresented oversensitive? Are you concerned about the media image of a group to which you have personal ties?

Realism and Ratings

A recent television movie, <u>Silent Witness</u>, depicted the fictional trial of three men suspected of gang rape. During the course of the trial the defense lawyer continually harassed the victim about her alcoholism and mental illness. The lawyer persuaded the jury that the woman was drunk at the time of the rape and therefore left herself open to sexual advances.

California state law makes this line of defense illegal. A rape victim's past cannot be used as evidence against her unless she has a history of extreme sexual promiscuity. But a rape victim who is unaware of her rights might be deterred from reporting the crime after viewing such harsh treatment. This type of media portrayal perpetuates society's attitude that a victim sexually provokes the rapists into committing the crime.

When dealing with an issue as sensitive as rape, television programmers should strive for realism rather than ratings. The media reflect and shape this country's values. Many stereotypes have become intrinsic to our culture with the help of repeated false characterization in television and movies.

Research indicates that almost half of the rapes in the United States go unreported. Victims are often too humiliated to seek legal action, said Delinda Rounsville, a counselor at the San Jose Women's Alliance.

Television programs should be more sensitive to a rape victim's fragile psychological state. <u>Silent Witness</u> and shows of its kind might confirm a victim's fears that she is the criminal. A woman may continue to suffer in silence rather than face society's ridicule.

This silence is not only detrimental to a victim's mental health, it hinders the judiciary's attempts to protect her rights and increase the number of rape convictions. Many people who deal with rapists and their victims believe that increased convictions will lower the general incidence of rape, Rounsville said.

"The only way the legal system is going to change is by victims speaking out," she said.

In one landmark case, a rape victim sued her landlord on the grounds that her apartment was unsafe. After her rape, the woman discovered that the previous tenant had also been assaulted. Both times, the rapist entered the apartment through a window with a broken lock. The woman won her case.

The media need to take cases such as this into consideration before airing shows that deal with rape. Most television programs are now designed to increase public awareness that rape is a violent crime and not a sexual act, Rounsville said. Talk shows feature interviews with victims and psychologists, and David Soul recently starred in another television movie as a convicted rapist who was rehabilitated through a prison support group, she said. However, the media should not assume that one responsible show cancels out one dramatization. Emotions sometimes speak louder than facts.

164 / PART THREE: WRITING ACROSS THE CURRICULUM

THE READER'S TURN:

1. What is this writer's objection to the television movie? Does her objection seem justified?
2. Does this writer succeed in making you look at the issue from the point of view of the victim?
3. In the "landmark case" this writer cites, do you think it was fair to blame the landlord?
4. Sometimes it seems as if Americans have resigned themselves to horrendous crime rates as facts of life. Does this paper point toward effective corrective action?
5. Network executives tend to defend crime shows as entertainment or escape. Do you agree with them? Look at some key examples to justify your position.

The Last Temptation

"The dual substance of Christ--the yearning, so human, so superhuman, of man to attain to God, . . ." Who can read these opening lines from the prologue of Nikos Kazantzakis' Last Temptation of Christ without feeling the stirring of inscrutable mysteries within their own soul? In all of his work, Kazantzakis struggles with the profound mysteries of God, and nature, and humanity. The pages are splashed with his blood and tears. He was a great and daring soul, on a merciless quest--and never less than honest.

Zorba, Saint Francis, Report to Greco, Temptation--the love and anguish in these books never fails to touch me in some deeply mysterious way. For me they are dense with feverish images, mysterious nostalgic longing, and powerful passions. They are ensigns of the passage of a hero-- especially, Last Temptation. As Kazantzakis said: "This book is not a biography; it is the confession of every man who struggles."

Kazantzakis' masterpiece was brought to the screen by Martin Scorcese, arguably America's most talented and sensitive filmmaker. But the film had sparked tremendous controversy even before it was released--especially from fundamentalist Christians, who wanted it suppressed, and even destroyed. 20,000 people had showed up at Universal studios to protest it the day before it opened. Why? Kazantzakis is the most sincerely spiritual man I've ever read. Scorcese studied for the Catholic priesthood. What's going on here?

I went to the first showing. At the time, it didn't seem beyond the realm of possibility that there might not be a second.

My friend Don and I arrived at the Northpoint Theater at 9:00 a.m. The tickets didn't go on sale until 12:30. Except for a jittery theater manager and a small army of security guards in the lobby, we were the only ones around. That surprised us, and I think it surprised the security people too. Every once in a while one would stick his head out the door for a bewildered glance up and down the street.

About 9:30, Rebecca, a reporter for KCBS radio showed up.

"Are you guys in line for the movie?" she asked.

It was kind of hard to tell. There was a bus stop there. We might have been waiting for a bus in the only spot out of the wind. Like us, she was expecting a big crowd; gangs of fervent believers clashing over fundamental philosophical issues. Devout people with deeply held religious convictions on one side, and equally devout civil libertarians on the other. She was disappointed and interviewed us instead. I told her I thought it was a great book, and that, with all the hype, I had expected there would be a crowd already--something like the opening of a new <u>Star Wars</u> movie, maybe. Don said he was against prior censorship. It wasn't much of a story.

About 10:00 a few more people joined us in line, and the first protester showed up. I wasn't sure he was a protester at first. He didn't have a placard and he didn't harangue us for our intended patronage of a blasphemy. He stood on the corner for a while looking impatiently up and down the street. I thought he might be a businessman waiting for his ride to work. He peevishly picked lint off his blue blazer. He smoothed down his huge blond pompadour. Finally he shrugged, went to his car, and put on a sandwich board he got from the trunk. On the front it said: "Only Jesus' Blood Can Save!"; on the back: "Prepare to meet thy God.--Amos 4:12."

I think it was almost 11:00 before the first TV crew showed up. Our second protester had arrived, seemingly out of nowhere, and he didn't need a bullhorn. He bellowed like a bull. He leafleted everybody in sight. His message was that he had uncovered a sinister satanic conspiracy. Only a fool could dismiss the evidence. Robert De Niro, who had played the devil in <u>Angelheart</u>, had also played the lead in <u>Taxi Driver</u>--a Scorcese film. It was <u>Taxi Driver</u> that inspired John Hinkley to attempt to assassinate Ronald Wilson Reagan, who has six letters in each of his names. 666: the mark of the beast.

By 11:30 there were about a hundred people in line. All of a sudden there were TV crews everywhere, and just as suddenly the protesters appeared. The anti-protesters appeared. In the space of a few minutes the sidewalk was mobbed. People poured in from every direction--people and more people. A choir warmed up on the corner next to a guy who had dragged in a twenty-foot cross mounted on a little roller skate. When the cameras were on, he spewed fire and brimstone like Vesuvius—when they were off, he fell strangely silent. An emaciated priest with thin, hunched shoulders, and a face that seemed to be carved out of pink wood, shepherded a group of older women through the midst of the chaos. They huddled together making little cooing sounds like a flock of roosting hens. Two self-righteous young men engaged in a loud, if murky, debate. Placards bristled in the crowd like the spines of a threatened porcupine.

I lost track of how many TV crews had shoved a microphone under my nose. Channel 7, Channel 5, Channel 11, or was it 36? I was starting to get good at my little speech. I found myself adding little gestures and dramatic pauses for the camera.

Faith (I'm not making this up, that really was her name), the reporter from Channel 2, informed us that the satellite feed had taken our image across the country--to Orlando, Florida, for some reason.

"You're famous in Orlando," she said.

After we had our tickets, the line shifted to the other side of the building, but to get there we had to wade through the Hispanic ladies on their knees, clutching their crucifixes. At last, after a frisking in the lobby, we were admitted to the theater. Inside, the prospective audience was immediately anesthetized by a deafening muzak version of the Hawaiian Wedding Song. A row of surly security guards were posted between the audience and the screen, just in case. I felt lucky to get inside without being spit on.

Oh yes, what about the movie? I have to tell the truth--I was disappointed. Ironically, I thought the last 40 minutes or so--the crucifixion and the infamous temptation sequence--were the best parts, but they didn't approach the intensity of the novel.

I couldn't escape the feeling that Scorcese had chickened out. The whole thing was anemic. Nothing to get excited about. At first I couldn't understand what was making these people so upset. On the way out, one of the crowd gave me a clue. It was an older man, maybe in his sixties, red-faced and sputtering with outrage.

"That's disgusting," he choked. "There's no way Jesus was a wimp like that!"

Wimp? I was beginning to see the problem. This Christ was not all-knowing and beatific. This was not the softly glowing, antiseptic Christ of serene self-confidence and divine purity. This Christ was plagued by fear, and desire, and doubt--especially, doubt. This Christ was struggling desperately, with all the ambiguities and paradoxes of life--just like us. The old fellow didn't like the idea. He couldn't stand it. This Christ was uncertain, and our Father in heaven could never be that. Even at sixty, he wanted his Father to make it all right.

But it will never be all right. Life will never be simple and clear and easy, and Daddy can't fix it for you, once you grow up. Christ showed us the road to salvation, but the name of that road is sacrifice--sacrifice of our childish, comforting fantasies. It is not an easy road. It is steep, and rugged, and spotted with the drops of blood, of those who have traveled it. It is painful, and dark, and terrifying, and yes--confusing, but it is only here, that we truly follow in the footsteps of Christ.

An all-knowing Christ has no value to humanity. Unless Christ was tempted, he didn't conquer temptation. Unless he was terrified of the cross, he was no hero. Unless he was filled with doubt, he accomplished nothing. But, if we believe Christ triumphed, we have a model before us. And if we are to be saved, we must take up the cross--and follow.

> Understandably, this terrifying church has few advocates. Most people prefer a less demanding faith.
> Outside the theater, the circus was still going on: the moviegoers, the protesters, the protesters protesting the protesters, the media. If anything, the frenzy had increased. We got through the doors, but we couldn't get any further. An ocean of agitated humanity was surging against the front of the theater. It was impossible to make ourselves heard over the furious din. The intersection was gridlocked. A woman in a floral-print Mumu was hanging out of her car window taking pictures.

THE READER'S TURN:

1. In the opening paragraphs, this writer pays tribute to an admired author. What keynotes are struck here? How do they echo later in the paper?
2. The early wait at the movie theater is different from what the writer had expected; it is anticlimactic. Why? What is the effect on the reader? What is the writer's treatment of the protesters when they finally appear? Do they become real? Do you think the picture we get of them here is fair?
3. What is the role of the media in this sequence of events?
4. This viewer found the actual movie disappointing. Why? Nevertheless, the whole experience causes the writer to make some basic points about different attitudes toward religion. What are the basic points?
5. In some societies, censorship is a daily fact of life. Why do cases of attempted censorship become big media events in our society? Do you think there is a special justification for censorship where religious subjects are concerned?

WRITING TOPICS 9

Increasingly the media shape our view of the world. Critics claim that what many Americans know about history, politics, law, or the rest of the world is mainly what they learn via the tube. Not surprisingly, people who take the media seriously are concerned to make us better informed newspaper readers, more critical and selective television viewers, and more discriminating consumers of Hollywood entertainment. How observant and critical are you as a consumer of media fare? (Start a viewer's log to gather material for papers on topics like the following.)

1. The Daily Diet: Study a type or genre of program that is a staple in the regular diet of television fare. What is a soap opera—what is the secret of its appeal? What are the hallmarks of a B-movie? How do television documentaries deal with the subject of war? What genre is represented by classics like *I Love Lucy* or *The Honeymooners*, and what was the secret of their success?

2. Crime Does Not Pay: Do crime shows perpetuate (or create) stereotypes about crime and criminals? How do they picture blacks, Hispanics, Asians, women? What kind of law enforcement officers do these programs glorify? Focus on one major issue that should concern alert viewers; provide detailed vivid examples.

3. Just the News, Please: Conservatives accuse the news media of a liberal bias; liberals claim that the media are in the pockets of the business people who own them. Study political commentary or interviews on television. Can you identify and document political leanings, biases, or agendas? What seem to be the political sympathies or inclinations of prominent newscasters, commentators, or interviewers?

4. Consumer Beware: Study a typical day of TV commercials as research for drawing up a composite portrait of the typical consumer as envisioned by television advertisers. What are the mythical consumer's needs, preferences, vulnerabilities, and fantasies? What estimate do the commercials imply of the viewer's standards or intelligence? Use striking authentic examples.

5. For Music Lovers: Parents, ministers, and critics have been astounded and appalled by what they see and hear on MTV. How justified are their objections? What would you tell them if asked for your opinion?

10
Social Issues: The Unfinished Agenda

We often hear people complaining of public apathy toward the social issues of our time. And yet we live in a society where an army of social scientists studies the causes and symptoms of poverty and crime. The media feature exposés and background studies of teenage pregnancy, child abuse, drug addiction, or the homeless mentally ill. Often, apparently, neither the ample available data nor the media circus surrounding a hot current topic translates into a sense of personal commitment or personal responsibility.

The student writers in this group do not write about the issues of our society as outside observers. They offer us the personal testimony of people directly involved. Do you think they succeed in breaking through the crust of apathy?

Pink Collar Workers

Some of the strongest writing in today's composition classes is done by young women in the process of discovering the history and the challenges of the women's movement. This writer's testimony helps readers see how the issue of women's rights may look to the coming generation.

Between Two Worlds

Many people seem to think that racism is yesterday's issue and that the Civil Rights movement has gone too far. But as the testimony of this writer shows, race is an unresolved issue for many young Americans.

A Complex Issue

Much brave talk about the abortion issue is done by people not biologically equipped to bear children. This writer does not preach about the topic from a soapbox but instead speaks from relevant personal experience.

Rape

"I figured the police would turn it around" and start blaming the victim. In this paper, the intended victim talks about the psychological aftermath of her experience.

Pictures from My Mother's Trip to Hell

People battling mental illness find themselves at every turn struggling against ignorance, complacency, taboos, and misguided good intentions. For the concerned reader, this paper traces the route through anger and despair to understanding and compassion.

Pink Collar Workers

Many women, like myself, when hearing the word "feminist" try to stay as far away as possible. Images of protests, marching libbers on the war path, and loud radical women come to mind. I held many misconceptions about the Women's Movement. I thought that as many as 80% of these women hated men. Since some of the most active feminists have been outspoken lesbians, the media have exaggerated this part of the feminist movement. Like many other people, I tended to stay away from anything having to do with homosexuality. However, after having a Women's Studies class, I feel I understand much more about what the movement is trying to accomplish. After seeing facts and statistics on the injustices that women are faced with, I can say without a doubt that I, too, am a feminist.

Using the true definition of a feminist--anyone who believes in equal rights between men and women--is saying that a feminist need not be a woman but can also be a man. You might ask why a man would want to identify himself as a feminist. Besides the obvious reason of being fair, men, too, can benefit from what the movement is trying to do. Since there is sexism--discrimination of one sex over another--today, many women aren't paid as much, or they are in what is called pink collar jobs (secretaries, teachers, clerical workers, etc.). All of these jobs don't pay as well as the typical male career. In effect, since women aren't making as much, the financial burden is placed solely on men. Some men have to find a better job or take on two jobs. One goal of the Women's Movement is to eliminate male-identified women, and to encourage women to be self-identified women--women that respect and shape themselves according to their own values.

A conference at Seneca Falls in 1848 represented the first wave of feminism in the U.S. A small assembly affirmed their belief in equality of men and women and wanted to pursue the struggle for sex equality. The first wave of feminism was led by women activists of the anti-slavery movement. Some extremely outspoken feminists were Susan B. Anthony, Elizabeth Cady Stanton, Lucretia Mott, and Matilda Joslyn Gage. They all agreed that the women's right to vote was the first priority. This was not achieved until 1920, after some seventy-two years of struggle. There was only one single woman of those who had attended the Seneca Falls Convention who was still alive to cast her first vote. The following quote is from Elizabeth Cady Stanton, writing to Lucretia Mott:

> The more I think on the present condition of woman, the more I am oppressed with the reality of her degradation. The laws of our country, how unjust they are! Our customs, how vicious! What God has made sinful, both in man and woman, custom has made sinful in woman alone.

The next quote is from Susan B. Anthony from a letter she wrote to her sister, urging her to join the movement:

> We need not wait for one more generation to pass away in order to find a race of women worthy to assert the humanity of women; and that is all we claim to do.

I grew up with a best friend whose parents, especially her mother, would tell her that as long as she found a "good" man, she wouldn't have to worry about college or a good job. At school, my friend took classes like sewing and cooking. I always felt really bad for her because my parents were exactly the opposite. They always encouraged me to take pre-college classes and to first finish college before settling down. Their philosophy was that I should first be strong in myself and have a good job then think about marriage. That way, if something was to end the marriage (divorce, death), I could take care of myself. While we were growing up, I was in after-school sports, but my friend wasn't allowed to so she'd go home and wait for me.

Everywhere we look, billboards and movies convey a message of how a woman should look and should be. I once saw an ad selling perfume where there was a beautiful woman's head attached to a snake's body with hands open towards a man. The caption read, "Dare to be tempted."

This ad implied that women are like the snake in the garden trying to tempt and deceive men. If people keep seeing ads and movies like that, they will eventually begin to believe them.

Today's women of the second wave of feminism are asking how long before the struggle for equal rights--which has been pursued by feminists every year since 1920--is won. While women have won important rights during the past, some of these rights are still under challenge (e.g. abortion). Statistics show that men's incomes have increased by about 5% over women's during the same period in which women supposedly have been making more marked advances toward equality than before. So are women more liberated now than before? Until men and women promote support towards women's issues, there will not be any advances. Even if an issue doesn't affect you directly, feminists need to be supportive of each other if any advancements are to be made.

THE READER'S TURN:

1. This paper starts with doubts and misgivings. Does this beginning weaken the paper?

2. The second paragraph talks about men and their relationship to the feminist movement. Do you think this is good strategy? For you, is the writer's perspective here new or unusual?

3. The main part of the paper moves through a look at history, through the author's experiences while growing up, to a look at media images. What does each of these parts contribute to the paper as a whole? (How would the paper change if one of these were missing?) Which affected you most strongly and why?

4. What is the tone and message in the conclusion? Are you satisfied with it? Are you disappointed by it?

5. This writer cared strongly about her subject. Prepare a reply spelling out how you feel about the issue and how you respond to the writer's plea.

Between Two Worlds

I find it hard to write about myself because I am going through a period of extreme self-evaluation. I come from what might have been an ordinary black family, except that one of my father's parents was white. In fact, my older sister usually passes for white. (Some blacks are foolish enough to consider an appearance like hers a status symbol.) I, however, am brown-complexioned, and I have a younger brother who is somewhere in between. These simple facts about my ancestry have left me confused and stranded in a twilight zone between two worlds.

When I was in elementary school, people thought I might be black or Mexican or Indian, and it was here that my problems began. My older sister was thought of as white by her teachers as well as her friends. When I came up to her to ask her a question during recess, she would tell me to leave, and as I did I could hear her friends inquire, "Who was that little black kid?" I remember one day when my sister came home almost crying, making my mother tell me, "Leave your sister alone at school; she's big and you are little!" This, I discovered later, was not even half the truth. I have often in my later life been enraged at my sister, and we have never felt close.

I remember several incidents that helped me see the truth about "race relations." Once my family was traveling across the country to South Carolina to visit relatives. I recall our going into Mississippi and stopping at a small broken-down gas station. We waited and waited for service. My father even backed up the car and went forwards to the pump again to make the bell ring a second time. I remember the attendant, wearing a white tee shirt and open red-checkered flannel jacket, leaning back in his chair, looking out at us, and then continuing to read his <u>Field and Stream</u> magazine. I asked my father what the problem was, and he replied that it must be closing time. I suspiciously looked out of the back window as we pulled away. I saw another car pull up with a white driver, and the attendant, throwing down his magazine, jogged out to pump gas.

Even at this early age, I knew why. Although my parents never made any noise about it, I knew why. I was always a logical kid. I never believed in Santa Claus. I always had that knack for putting two and two together.

Fortunately, some happy years for a time made me forget my problems. We had moved to a small town where the people and the schools were mostly white. I made friends and became popular among my peers. I was elected class president in the sixth grade. However, shortly after, things changed. When we entered the seventh grade, most boys and girls became interested in each other. Naturally, my white friends started to date the girls they had known since kindergarten. It is not hard to guess who was left out. Perhaps this was partly by choice, since I have always been shy and still am. Or was my shyness a product of my situation? Once my best friend, who was white, asked me to invite a girl who was also white to a school dance. She said no, but, being young and naive, she also told me why. I never got over the experience, and I never asked a girl, white or black, to a dance again.

When we moved again, to a larger city, I discovered the flip side of my problem. The high school I went to was attended by many minority students, including many blacks. Because I did not "act black" (whatever that means), and because I did not look completely black, the black students gave me a very bad time. I had no black friends and only a few white "surface" friends (the type who when the weekend came disappeared). I never had a real girlfriend, and I can count the real dates I had on the fingers of one hand.

Now that I am in college, I am supposed to be open-minded and liberal, but my early experiences have molded by mind into a hard, thick cast of cement that will be difficult to break. I feel trapped in the twilight zone between two worlds. I am striving to find my own world, even if it means being there by myself.

THE READER'S TURN:

1. Polemics on the race issue often start with a strong denunciation of white callousness and oppression. How is this paper different? What tone does the writer set in the introduction?

2. Many people have ambivalent feelings about their background or their families—mixed feelings of love and hate, or of loyalty and rebellion. Where do this writer's ambivalent feelings show most strongly or most directly?

3. To some readers of this paper, the paragraph about the stop at the gas station has seemed symbolic or revealing. Why or how?

4. People who are unhappy or deprived often feel a strong need to point the finger at those who are to blame. Does this writer blame other people? How or where?

5. Does the conclusion this writer reaches in the final paragraph seem logical or inevitable to you? Assume you are a teacher, a counselor, or a friend. Prepare a letter in which you reply to this paper.

A Complex Issue

After I had had the flu for weeks and shown no signs of getting better, my mother became suspicious. She came into my room with a glass of grape juice and crushed ice (the only thing I could keep down) and asked me if there was any way I could be pregnant. I was fourteen. My mother calmly sat there on the edge of my bed, stroking my hair, waiting for me to get up the courage to nod.

I had known how babies were made for a long time; I grew up on a farm, after all. But, I somehow didn't know it could happen to me. I guess I hadn't thought about it at all. My boyfriend was older. He was in college, and this sort of thing wasn't new to him. But, I guess he hadn't thought about it either.

My mom took me to a doctor. The doctor, a young man, recommended an abortion. He said that's what he'd do if it happened to his girl. Since abortions weren't legal in our state at that time, he gave my mother the name of a clinic in the big city on the other side of the state line.

My boyfriend, a good Catholic boy, did the right thing. He asked me to marry him. I thought about being kicked out of cheerleading, having to quit school (pregnant girls didn't go to school then), and losing my future in a pile of diapers and his dirty socks. He thought about having to go to work, quitting the golf team, and breaking his mother's heart by letting her know what he'd been up to. My mom didn't even think about it. She took me to the city.

It was an easy mess to clean up: like sucking up dog hair off the carpet. I heard the same vacuum cleaner sounds, and it was over.

My life was saved. I went back to being a kid. I went back to school, back to cheerleading, back to getting good grades so I could go to college. I always knew I'd go to college.

I hadn't even thought about having the baby and putting it up for adoption. To a fourteen-year-old, nine months is the same as forever. Yet, sometimes in the shadows of my dreams, I still see that worm-like embryo in the vacuum where it lies hidden in blood and tears. The part of me where this horrible secret swirls is darkened as I live with the guilt of ending a life.

I like my life. The boyfriend was replaced. I met the man I'm still married to. When I was eighteen, we were married. I have a boy and a girl and a lot to prove. I try to make up in these two for what I did to that one. We have a good and happy life. I know that if I had had that baby when I was fourteen, my life would be very different. So on one hand, I'm thankful for the decision my mom helped me make.

On the other hand, I live with the guilt. I remember running out of a class where the abortion issue was being discussed. The years have done a lot of healing. I can talk about it now, though I always feel shame and worry what people who know will think of me.

I know of a woman who's had four abortions. She uses them as a form of birth control. She's married and her husband doesn't want children. I wonder how she feels. I wonder what she sees in her dreams.

I know of an infertile woman who's been trying to adopt a child for six years. I wonder how she feels about the soaring abortion rates.

I get letters from Planned Parenthood asking me to donate money so impoverished women will have the freedom to end unwanted births. Though I believe in reproductive freedom, I can't send money. I have also been asked to join pro-life groups. I can't do that either. An unwanted pregnancy is a two-edged sword that cuts deep either direction it's moved. Planned Parenthood and other people for reproductive freedom want to slice one way while right-to-lifers want to slice the other way. Either way the sword cuts the mother's life, the wound leaves scars. Abortion is a complex issue.

THE READER'S TURN:

1. Up until the actual procedure, this writer tells a story that at one time was not uncommon. How many details can you identify that contribute to a sense of *déjà vu?*

2. What is different about the author's account of the actual procedure? How does it affect you as a reader?

3. Unlike people who write on this issue with self-righteousness, this writer discusses her experience with powerful mixed feelings, torn between "on the one hand" and "on the other hand." Do you understand how she feels? Can you explain her feelings to an outsider?

4. In the final paragraphs, this writer spells out her stand on the issue. How is what she says different from the familiar arguments of the pro-life and pro-choice factions?

5. Do you agree with the writer? Write a reply to her in which you defend your own point of view.

Rape

There are situations that come up in people's lives, situations that, no matter what a person says or does there is nothing he or she can do to stop them. These situations can leave a person feeling so vulnerable that just to go outside is a terrifying experience. A person can be stripped of every ounce of dignity and pride that ever existed in her. A person can go from being normal, happy, and trusting, and in just a matter of seconds all that can be ripped away. All of these feelings can be caused by one person, one very sick person, in the act of rape.

It was a very hot night in May of last year. I had left my window open a little way because my room was so stuffy from the night's heat. I guess it was around three or four in the morning; I don't really remember exactly. I felt safe, as I always did. I was in my house, in my room, in my bed and I was asleep.

Something startled me and I woke up. I opened my eyes and I saw a man leaning in through my window. I never thought at first that it wasn't someone whom I knew. It was dark and I was still very much groggy with sleep so I wasn't thinking too quickly. I immediately thought it was a friend from work. The friend I thought of was supposed to be out of town, but again I wasn't thinking too clearly. Thinking he was a friend, I sat up in bed and told him that he had scared me, and I asked what he was doing in my window. He was unable to pull himself all the way in. Once I had sat up, he could reach me; he grabbed me by the shoulders and used me as a brace to pull himself the rest of the way in. He proceeded to push me back down on my bed and he was kissing my face and his hands, his hands were everywhere--well, at least he was trying to get them everywhere. My room was spinning; I didn't know what was happening nor did I know what to do. I kept pushing his hands away and at the same time trying to push him off of me. He was dirty and grimy and I could smell the awful mixture of chips and beer on his breath. Finally I got a good grip on him, and I pushed him with all of my 3:00 a.m. strength against his chest. That moment was the first time I realized that I didn't know this man. He had a disgustingly thick mound of hair on his chest, and no one I knew had that much.

It was that reality that finally woke me up to what this man was actually attempting to do. I sat up and told him I was going to count to three and if he wasn't gone I would scream. He responded with, "Wait, can't we talk about this?" I couldn't believe it: He was trying to rape me, and he wanted to discuss the fact.

I only had to count up to one. He flew out of my window so fast, if I would have blinked I would have missed it.

Afterwards I felt guilty, used, betrayed, but most of all dirty. The next day and for a while after I was even self-conscious of the way I dressed. Everything we hear on television about how rape victims feel I was feeling. Even though I was lucky enough to stop him before the actual act of rape, I was still raped. I was raped of my dignity, my pride, my trust. I'm the type of person who hates to be afraid of anything; that is what angered me the most. It's not as bad for me now, but for the first few months afterwards I was afraid of my own shadow.

I never screamed, I never called the police, and I never even told my family. I don't know why I didn't scream. I didn't think about the police until after he was long gone. I figured the police would turn it around and start asking me why I didn't have a screen and a lock on my window. I couldn't describe the man because of the darkness, so I knew they would never be able to catch him. I still haven't told anyone in my family because, I guess, inside I'm a little embarrassed about it still.

I now have a screen and a lock on my window. I also sleep with a baseball bat next to my bed.

THE READER'S TURN:

1. In the opening paragraph, the writer tries to sum up the point of her story. What is she saying?
2. Lawyers try to undermine the credibility of damaging witnesses. Does this writer's account of her experience ring true? What makes it sound like a true story?
3. What are the writer's feelings about the police? Do you sympathize?
4. In the final paragraphs, the writer is redefining and rethinking the term *rape*. How?
5. Is there anything to be learned from this writer's account of her experience? If anyone asked you what the answer is, what would you say?

Pictures from My Mother's Trip to Hell

My father, my younger brother and I drove to see her in our blue Toyota, a car that I remember as having a particular pull; I mean when I was riding in it, I felt as if the cab of the car must be leaning back in the force of the road wind, and the engine felt right under my feet. I could feel how hard the engine pulled to bring me to my destination.

This morning I called my brother, now twenty years old, and I asked him what he remembered about Mom and the time when she was sick. It was strange to him that he could not remember much. I was having the same problem. Both of us had only snippets of memory, family memory, about this period of time that lasted over ten years. He remembered drawing pictures for her while she was in the hospital. I remember a particular visit.

I did not know what to expect at the hospital, not bars on the windows or heavy doors, but I was led into a quiet, carpeted hallway. My mother must have hugged Jason and me, but I don't remember. I was twelve; he was six. She didn't seem embarrassed to be there. In fact, she talked about the deer that came up to her window to graze in the evenings. We walked to a small, overgrown courtyard toward the front of the hospital grounds. Today I can compare it to an English-style garden, very symmetrical, with small plots inlaid into the cement. On one side was a very high wall, and a terrace extended into the courtyard. It was all as overgrown as the inlaid plots were. I wondered if deer came to the top of the wall and if patients, like the few I saw wandering apart from us, ever tried to climb it.

My mother sat with my father on a bench while Jason and I walked around one of the inlaid gardens. I could not look at my mother very closely. Her face was puffy and her eyes were blank. To walk this small distance she had had to lean on my father and take very slow steps. She had just had her first series of shock treatments. She had gained about twenty pounds as a result of the heavy medication that she needed to, to what--I am still not sure. I did not cry. I felt as if I were looking at someone other than my mother, but I could not have been sure that this woman was not now my new mother, that she had changed into this slow creature for good.

The earliest memory I have of my mother comes from winter mornings when I'd wake to the smell of coffee and to the sound of the heater pinging, and I would see her under a small light where she sat to knit or read the paper. She had such a warm light that I loved to get up to her cozy presence. Certainly it had taken many years for the change that was so deep to occur.

She has since been diagnosed as manic depressive, and to my impressionistic memory, this makes sense. She had trouble coping in spurts. Sometimes I'd come home from school and she would be sitting in the corner of the living room sofa crying. Sometimes she would be sleeping. Music disturbed her and I always seemed to turn it on too loud. Though sometimes she orchestrated me in preparing the carrots, and potatoes, assembling the roast and vegetables, in time I became the main cook.

She would sleep through dinner if we did not wake her, which was difficult, and bring her to the table. I cooked soups with hamburger; I broiled cheeseburgers for my dad and brother. I even came to imitate her chili pretty well. But in our household, dinner time was always a tense affair. My mother's psychiatrist would call in the middle of it and Mom would leave the table, take the phone into her room, and talk to him. She usually came back to us tearful. We never asked her what he had said.

Through this man, my parents became involved in Primal Therapy. My mother's group therapy session would come over on a Saturday afternoon and "work out" in our backyard. My father was a member of this group at one point, but to save his sanity, I liked to think, he stopped. When he did belong to this group, he stored an old twin mattress in our shed, and the group members would come over, have a glass of wine, and go out into the yard, armed with broomsticks, and they would beat on this mattress as hard as they could, shouting as they flailed, "I hate you, mother," or "I hate you, father." There were next-door neighbor kids my age, and when the session began, their parents would make them come indoors.

One evening when my father was driving me to the library to study in that blue Toyota that seemed to work so hard to overcome inertia, my dad tried to assure me, "Your mom is getting better; it looks like this time she's really feeling better." We had had this conversation several times. This time I said, as we sat at an intersection, "No, she's never going to get better; you've been saying it for years and she never gets better." He dropped me off at the arch of the library where my friends were waiting.

In high school, I had my friends to comfort me when something went wrong, although I didn't speak much about my mother to my friends. No one wanted to believe that a person who looked normal, who didn't tear her hair or have wild eyes, could be mentally ill. I thought much of the time that she brought her problem upon herself, but her outbursts of anger and tears were more than "bad moods."

One night, after a particularly bad argument about boyfriends and staying out, I stomped into my room. But Mom wasn't finished. She stormed into my room and demanded that I move out. I was used to these outbursts, and I knew I must remain calm. The calmer I stayed, the closer she came to exploding. I began to gather up some things. Maybe it would be better if I left. And then she began to yell at me about what a horrible person I had let myself become. She cursed me. I tried to ignore her. Maybe I even reached for the phone, but somehow she had the phone and she tugged at it, she wanted to rip it out of the wall, but for all her anger she couldn't do it, so she slammed the heavy phone into the wall, into the mural I had painted in watercolor. The anger I felt toward this person who used to be mother did not let go of me for many years.

Today, eight years later, I went into the room at my mother's house where my baby girl was sleeping. It was dinner time. Together we peeked out of the bedroom door into the early evening sitting room where my mother, grandma, sat in the small glow of her lamp, knitting, concentrating on her work.

My mother has been to the hell that exists on earth, and she's back. She does not talk about it. She still struggles with depression. She will take lithium, the chemical cure for manic depressives, for the rest of her life. She tries; she wants badly to leave behind the drugs that control her mood swings. My mom has complete care of my daughter at least two days a week. She and my father are still married, miraculously. She is also active in Buddhism, where she helps people who have difficulties in their lives to cope. I am proud, no longer frightened of my mother, no longer compassionless to her or anyone else's struggle to make sense out of the world. Above all, I am no longer angry. I love my mother more than ever.

THE READER'S TURN:

1. Brainstorm the subject of mental illness. What images, ideas, or associations come to your mind?

2. The subject of mental illness is shrouded in prejudice, taboos, and good intentions. Very few people take the actual trip to a mental hospital. What did this writer see there?

3. How does one cope as the relative of a mentally ill person? Trace this writer's own journey—her memories and feelings.

4. People faced with apparently insurmountable afflictions often lose hope. Do you think this paper will give them courage?

5. Do you have a story about a severe affliction that leads to a happy ending? Or do you have a story about adversity that does not have a happy end?

WRITING TOPICS 10

Much of the writing we encounter aims at alerting us to unresolved social issues, analyzing their roots, and advocating solutions. Some of the writers hew to the approved procedures and research methods of the social sciences. They study scientifically selected samples and discuss the meaning and validity of carefully researched statistics. Other writers let their conscience be their guide, appealing to our sense of responsibility or our compassion. How concerned and how well informed are you about some of the unresolved social issues of our time?

1. Getting the Facts: On subjects like the size of the homeless population, contradictory impressions abound. Try to get and interpret the best current statistics on this or a similar subject where numbers are often used to magnify or belittle the issue. Discuss the sources and reliability of your statistics. Break down your numbers into subcategories. (For instance, how many of the homeless are mentally ill, and how does anyone know? How many are men, women, children, families—and what do the numbers mean?)

2. Issues and Side Issues: Skeptics claim that issues like school prayer or the pledge of allegiance at the beginning of the school day are pseudo-issues designed to distract attention from the real problems that confront our society. Are such charges true, or do such symbolic issues have a genuine significance?

3. Victims' Rights: We are often told that our justice system goes overboard to protect those innocently accused but does little for the innocent victim. What is the nature—what are the origins, causes, prospects—of the victims' rights movement? Has it begun to make a difference for crime victims in your community or your neighborhood? Research the available literature; use firsthand investigation and interviews. Write to forewarn the potential victim.

4. Viewing with Alarm: People who try to counter public apathy on an issue dear to their hearts are often accused of being alarmists or extremists. Try to evaluate the validity of the claims made by people who speak up strongly on an issue like the following: animal rights, endangered species, discrimination against the disabled, censorship of textbooks, explicit sexual material on television, sexism in commercials. Present your findings for the benefit of the concerned voter.

5. Laissez-Faire: Do we need to do more as a society to deal with social problems that are the result of neglect or misguided policies? Or is the best solution to social problems to liberate personal initiative and encourage self-reliance? To which of these alternatives do you incline philosophically or temperamentally? Take a stand. Support your position with detailed current examples.

11
Literature: The Responsive Reader

Imaginative literature is a mirror that can tell us who we are, where we came from, and where we are headed. Poets and storytellers share with us their vision of reality as they take us into their personal world of thoughts and feelings. One major function of critical writing about literature is to guide us through that personal world, helping us see the world through the poet's or storyteller's eyes, helping us become more receptive and more responsive readers.

Today We Have Naming of Parts

Poets often do not give us a message in dry abstract words; instead, they make us ponder images and details rich in meaning. This student writer takes a close look at the images and feelings in two poems that "condemn our failure to see war as it is."

Kate Chopin: Precursor of Modern Literature

This short student paper looks at a recently rediscovered nineteenth-century writer of short stories as a precursor of twentieth-century realism.

Hemingway and the World of Illusion

For several generations of readers, Ernest Hemingway was one of the leading voices of postwar disillusionment. This student paper presents a close reading of a classic Hemingway story to discover what it can tell us about the role of illusions.

Ramona—Fact or Fiction?

This student paper focuses on a nineteenth-century work of popular historical fiction dealing with the fate of the California Indians during the transition from the earlier mission days under Mexican rule to rapidly increasing American settlement. The student writer compares fact and fiction as she checks the Romanticized picture painted in the novel with the views of latter-day historians.

Today We Have Naming of Parts

After the disillusioning experience of World War II, Henry Reed in "Naming of Parts" and Richard Eberhart in "The Fury of Aerial Bombardment" condemn and reject the horror of war. Both poems condemn our failure to see war as it is, attack our indifference, and reflect postwar anti-war feeling. We shall see that Eberhart's poem takes the attack on indifference one step further than Reed's poem does.

Henry Reed's "Naming of Parts" satirically attacks the callousness of the military. By using impersonal, neutral words and phrases ("Today we have naming of parts. / Yesterday we had daily cleaning"), the speaker satirizes how precise and impersonal these lessons are. The trainee learns a process, without being taught or made aware how terrible and ugly practicing that process is. References to "the lower sling swivel," "the upper sling swivel," and the "slings" describe machinery. Such references to mechanical parts evoke neutral or even positive feelings, since most machines are used for the good of humanity. This technical language conceals the horror of using this particular machinery. Saying that "you can do it quite easy / If you have any strength in your thumb" obscures the possibility that it might be difficult emotionally to gun down a fellow human being.

Reed uses a comparison to nature at the end of each stanza. Jumping from the mechanics of the gun to the beauty of the garden in consecutive sentences presents a contrast between the gun and the flower, the one a symbol of death and the other a symbol of life. The references in the first two stanzas stress the innocence of nature. The line "Japonica glistens like coral in all of the neighboring gardens" evokes an image of serenity and peace. The branches "with their silent and eloquent gestures" paint another image of bliss. The sterile descriptions of the gun and the beautiful descriptions of nature proceed in a point-counterpoint fashion.

Richard Eberhart's "The Fury of Aerial Bombardment" shares the theme of "Naming of Parts" in that both poems attack indifference to violence and suffering. By saying that "History, even, does not know what is meant," the poet seems to lament that even painful experience does not teach us to prevent the senselessness of war. We are "no farther advanced," making the poet ask: "Was man made stupid?" Here again, as in Reed's poem, technical, impersonal references to the "belt feed lever" and the "belt holding pawl" imply a criticism of the callousness with which people handle the subject of war. A lesson about a belt feed lever might be more instructive if the part were named the genocide lever, for instance.

However, "The Fury of Aerial Bombardment" contrasts with "Naming of Parts" because Eberhart goes beyond attacking human indifference by attacking divine indifference to the horror of war. The poet questions why God has not intervened to stop the aerial bombardment. The answer, that "the infinite spaces / Are still silent," is a criticism of God's looking passively upon "shock-pried faces." There are the faces of the people who have witnessed the horrors of the bombing but to whom God offers no respite. The poet seems to expect a thinking, feeling entity to intervene, but no such intervention takes place. Men still kill with "multitudinous will." In the third stanza, the poet asks: "Is God by definition indifferent, beyond us all?"

Both of these poems were written about forty years ago, yet their relevance remains undiminished today. In an age when we read daily of war and death, indifference is commonplace. The way in which a news reporter casually reads death tolls from Beirut is reminiscent of the cold, sterile wording of "Naming of Parts." The casual and callous projections of the cost in human lives of "winning" a nuclear war are another example of what is under attack in these poems. And people who ponder such atrocities as Auschwitz and Hiroshima have cause to question divine indifference, for the earth is long on suffering.

THE READER'S TURN:

1. Which of the brief quotations used by the student writer are especially instructive or revealing? Does the writer's interpretation of these quotations seem convincing or justified?

2. Do you get a feeling for the Reed poem as a whole? What, according to the student writer, is the "point-counterpoint" pattern in the poem?

3. According to this paper, how is the second poem similar? How is it different? Do you think it was good strategy on the student writer's part to deal with the Reed poem first and the Eberhart poem second?

4. Do you agree that the relevance of these poems "remains undiminished today"?

5. Find a poem about war (or peace) and show its relevance for today's reader.

Kate Chopin: Precursor of Modern Literature

Of the writers of the late nineteenth century, Kate Chopin is one that unfortunately has received very little recognition. It is only very recently that her writings have been collected and appraised as precursors of modern twentieth-century literature. "The Story of an Hour" and "A Pair of Silk Stockings" are two of her short stories that especially exemplify the traits of the realistic tradition.

One trend of the realistic writer has been to portray characters and common events of a bourgeois society. In "A Pair of Silk Stockings," the protagonist, Mrs. Sommers, is an ordinary middle-class housewife. The main action centers upon her unexpected possession of fifteen dollars and the means by which she spends it in one day. The main character of "The Story of an Hour" is also a middle-class woman, although the situation, which concerns her reaction to the false news of her husband's death, is somewhat more tragic.

The crucial, distinctive characteristic, however, of realistic literature is not the focus on common people and events but the manner in which the subjects are treated, with a basic lack of sentimentality and idealism. The most striking element in Kate Chopin's stories is the almost ruthless attempt on the part of the author to present a true picture of society as she sees it, ugly though it may be. In "A Pair of Silk Stockings," unaltruistic feelings of selfishness and competition are revealed in such a way as would, and presumably did, shock complacent Victorian readers. Little Mrs. Sommers at first entertains generous plans to spend all of the fifteen dollars on new clothes for her children: "The vision of her little brood looking fresh and dainty and new for once in their lives excited her and made her restless and wakeful with anticipation." But, ironically, once at the shops, she indulges in buying herself a pair of silk stockings, and then, carried away by the sense of luxury and not once hindered by a guilty conscience, goes on to spend the entire sum on herself. Materialism in society is well depicted by the scene of the mad rush of shoppers at the bargaining counter. Mrs. Sommers, herself, "could stand for hours making her way inch by inch toward the desired object that was selling below cost."

THE READER'S TURN:

1. *Sentimentality* and *realism* are key terms used by critics of fiction. What does this student writer do to define these terms and bring them to life for the reader?

2. Have you read any modern literature that shows an "almost ruthless attempt on the part of the author to show a true picture"? Describe an outstanding example.

3. Why do you think the "realistic tradition" became strong in twentieth-century literature? Do you yourself make a good reader for realistic fiction? Why or why not?

Hemingway and the World of Illusion

Much of Hemingway's work concerns our struggle to cope in a world that is painful when stripped of illusions. His short story, "In Another Country," drawing on the author's own experiences, centers on wounded soldiers in Italy in World War I. In the story, people use different devices or contrivances to give themselves the illusion of physical and psychological well-being. These illusions are created so that no one will have to face squarely the realities of deterioration and death. The author makes us see our human need for illusion by contrasts in images, settings, and characters.

The opening paragraphs of the story present several such contrasts. The story takes place in Milan in Italy during World War I. It is fall, it is cold, and "dark comes early." War, fall, dark, and cold are words that suggest death or the ceasing of activity. Contrasted with these images are electric lights that come on at dark to shed light to the streets and shops. Light is a life image. Electric lights resurrect the cold, dark, dead world, making it appear beautiful and pleasant. The artificial light softens the reality that without these human contrivances the world is a cold, dark place where people deteriorate and die.

We soon encounter another death image: Hanging outside the shops are various kinds of game. Even if the snow picturesquely powders the fur of the dead foxes and even if the wind stirs the feathers of the birds, the fact remains that the animals are dead. "The deer hung stiff and heavy and empty" is a terse, blunt description of death. However, in the next paragraph, the men choose to get to the hospital by walking over a bridge where a woman sells roasted chestnuts. She roasts them over a charcoal fire (another human invention) that sheds warmth and light amidst the cold and darkness of the surroundings. Since the chestnuts stay warm in the men's pockets, they have the feeling of well-being that warmth affords while they are walking the remainder of the way to the hospital.

There is an old notion that people go to hospitals to die. The initial description of the hospitals as "old and beautiful" lessens the natural terror one might feel of such an institution. However, the sentences that follow offer no such comfort but explain in matter-of-fact fashion that people usually walk in the front gate alive and are carried out dead, by way of a funeral procession starting in the courtyard of the "old and beautiful" hospital. The only obstacle to this natural progression of events seem to be the "machines" housed inside the new brick pavilions, to the side of the hospital, where the men go for physical therapy.

The doctor presiding over the pavilions perpetrates illusions of healing by making the patients believe that they will be completely cured. He offers hope, with his "healing machines" and glib talk, to those who will believe in the illusions. To those with doubts, the doctor shows photographs of cured wounds, pointing out how, by the miraculous powers of the machines, badly wounded bodies have been resurrected so that they function "better than ever."

The central character of the story would like to believe these illusions. He is a young man, and it is devastating to him to have to face the reality of being badly deformed for the rest of his life. He wants to believe that he will be cured but notices contradictions between what the doctor professes and the realities of the situation. The doctor tells him he will "play football again like a champion" in spite of the fact that he has no calf and a knee that refuses to bend after months of manipulation by the machines. He also observes that the photograph of a "cured" hand is only slightly larger than that of the withered hand of the major, another patient.

The major, who takes treatment next to the young man, provides the counterpoint to the young man's need for illusions. The major is an older man who knows that no one has control over death and infirmity. His young wife has unexpectedly died after only a few days of illness. No manufactured machine or medicine could help her while she was ill, and nothing can resurrect her after her death. The young wife's death has taken from him the last tiny shred of belief in illusions.

The major's point of view offers a startling contrast to that of the doctor. Throughout the story, the young man is caught between those who believe in illusions and those who discard illusion and attempt to live with blunt reality. He recognizes the foolishness and untruth of the doctor's illusions, but he also notices the bitterness and resignation of the major who has discarded all illusion. After his wife's death, the major returns to the hospital resigned to the fact that nothing we can do will delay, for long, death. He just sits on his therapy machine and stares out of the window. He seems to be marking time. He does not believe in the machines, yet he comes each day to use them.

Through the major's example and the many contrasts presented in "In Another Country," Hemingway makes us see that, although life based on illusion is dishonest, most of us cannot live as functioning human beings without some illusions. The blunt reality of death and infirmity is too painful and frightening for most human beings to face. Our capacity for illusion provides the minimum of hope we need to go on living.

THE READER'S TURN:

1. This writer is especially sensitive to rich suggestive images and revealing details in Hemingway's story. Discuss some striking examples. Which especially help you get in the spirit of the story?

2. This writer takes a close look at revealing contrasts between different impressions and between major characters. According to the student writer, what role do these contrasts play in the story?

3. According to the writer, illusion is the central theme of the Hemingway story. What does the student writer say about the role of this central theme in the story? Where and how does this paper deal with the theme?

4. This paper has an exceptionally clear-cut overall plan or strategy. What is it?

5. Hemingway's books about the psychological aftermath of war gained for him a huge following. To judge from this paper, would you make a good audience for Hemingway's writing? Why or why not?

Ramona—Fact or Fiction?

First published in 1884, Helen Hunt Jackson's Ramona is a work of historical fiction which dramatizes the plight of the Indian in early 1850s Southern California. In the course of the story, Jackson discusses three periods in California history: the days of the Franciscan-led mission system, the era of the Mexican ranchos, and the time of the great influx of American settlers following the Gold Rush. In some instances, the novel corroborates the work of historians; in other cases it sharply conflicts with scholarly accounts. Ultimately Jackson's book tells the reader more about the period in which it was written than about the periods it describes.

Ramona's plot is suspenseful and highly melodramatic. Sometime during the 1830s a Scottish adventurer falls in love with a Californian lady of the gente de razon and sails off in search of a fortune with which to found a rancho. He returns carrying a booty of precious gems to find her married to someone else, and thereupon begins a long slide into drunken dereliction which culminates in his marriage to an Indian woman. The Indian woman bears him a child named Ramona, whom the dying Scotsman deposits with the jewels in the arms of his former love. This Californian lady, who has had a miserable life in retribution for her unfaithfulness, dies shortly thereafter; and custody of the child and the precious stones transfers to her widowed sister, Senora Moreno. The Senora Moreno is a stern and pious woman, embittered at the decline of Mexican ascendance in the province, who agrees to the arrangement only at the insistence of her beloved Franciscan confessor, Father Salvierderra. She raises Ramona dutifully yet coldly, reserving all her love for her amiable but ineffectual son, Felipe. Ramona grows up to be beautiful, devout, and sweet-tempered despite the Senora's coldness. One summer, when Ramona is twenty, a band of Indians headed by the handsome and virtuous Alessandro Assis comes to the rancho to shear the Moreno sheep. Ramona and Alessandro fall in love and wish to marry. The Senora becomes infuriated at the prospect of a member of her family marrying an Indian. She threatens Ramona with a convent and disinheritance. Ramona runs away with Alessandro and shares the sad experiences of his people in the newly American California. The two are forced to move farther and farther east as the remaining Indian settlements are dispossessed of their lands; finally they live in isolation near the peak of San Jacinto mountain. There Alessandro slowly goes mad as a result of the suffering he has witnessed. A white settler brutally murders him during a misunderstanding over a horse. Lying delirious in an Indian mountain village, Ramona is rescued by Felipe, whose personality has been much improved by the recent death of his mother. He and Ramona marry and move to Mexico, where, along with the Scotsman's jewels, they live happily, yet thoughtfully ever after.

Although the bulk of the action in Ramona takes place following the American conquest of California, Jackson does give us her assessment of the mission system established by the Spanish Franciscans in 1769. Historical writers have expressed divergent opinions on the efficacy and benevolence of the missions. Writing in the dry tone of the social scientist, Sherburne Cook views the mission system as detrimental to Indian life and culture. He cites the group demographic response of a declining Indian population, primarily attributable to death by disease, and the numerous instances of flight by individual Indians. The mission economy was based on forced labor, not onerous in itself, but alien to those used only to the intermittent, seasonal efforts of an aboriginal society. The Indians' disinclination to perform this type of labor, says Cook, led to punishments that were often cruel and capricious. He argues that despite the missionaries' proselytizing, the Indians managed to retain the basic pattern of their old religious culture. Carey McWilliams takes Cook's criticism of the Franciscan missions even further to liken them to concentration camps in their conditions and effects.

Maynard Geiger presents mission life in more favorable terms. He uses statistics from Mission Santa Barbara to demonstrate that the Indians were not stampeded or coerced into the system. But because he accepts the Catholic premise that the missions' foremost duty was to save souls, he condones the fathers' use of force to bring fugitive neophytes back into it. Geiger portrays the atmosphere in the missions as easygoing yet industrious, with the Indians sometimes evincing special enthusiasm for labor projects. Although free to return to their villages at the end of the workday, the young men preferred to remain in the mission patio and entertain themselves with music, dancing, and games. The father corrected most offenses with verbal reproof; physical punishment was employed as a last resort and only after several warnings. Geiger feels that the Indians showed a fair affinity for the Catholic religion.

Jackson's portrait of mission life has more in common with Geiger's than with Cook's. For her, the glory of the missions was that they provided an ideal environment for fusion of the two best elements ever present in California: the dedication of the Franciscan father and the Indian's nobility of the soul. Ramona's most sympathetically-drawn characters are the priest Father Salvierderra and the Indian Alessandro. Father Salvierderra is over eighty years old at the time of the story, old enough to have been active throughout the heyday of the missions. Jackson portrays him as unfailingly devoted to the welfare of the Indians, pious, persevering, and universally respected. Even the stubborn Senora Moreno improves within the sphere of his kindly influence. Alessandro is similarly idealized and endowed with an improbable number of virtuous qualities; among them sober industriousness, loyalty, selflessness, wisdom, and an inherent appreciation of nature's wonders.

At their best, the missions allowed priests of the caliber of Father Salvierderra to instill into Indians like Alessandro a sense of industry, education, self-reliance, and the ability to live independently. Padre and Indian communed in a mutual aesthetic appreciation of beauty, particularly music. Jackson concedes, however, that mission reality did not always mirror the ideal. At one point Ramona and Alessandro discuss this issue, and he explains to her that some bad priests exploited the Indians or dragged them into the missions against their will. Occasionally Jackson mentions Indians who lack Alessandro's ambition and refinement. Whether she attributes this to the effect of American rapaciousness or whether such Indians existed even during the days of the missions is unclear. Nonetheless, the majority of the missions are shown to have been successful enterprises where the Franciscans grafted the European work ethic onto willing Indian converts. For Jackson, the musical evenings in the patio, even the Catholicism, merely provide a romantic backdrop to this inculcation. She may not add to our historical understanding of the California missions, but she does let us know what qualities she and her late-nineteenth century readers considered important.

Ramona's account of the Mexican rancho period confirms that of other writers in some particulars. John Hittell has described the ruinous effect of American land legislation on the rancheros. When we meet the Senora Moreno, she has lost most of her former holdings to American legal perfidy. Her horror at Ramona's marriage to an Indian underscores McWilliams' point about the race hatred of the California upper crust. The story of Ramona's Scottish father illustrates McWilliams' discussion of European adventurers who merged into Hispanic California society. Here the similarities end. McWilliams states that the rancheros plundered the secularized mission assets, and pauperized and peonized the Indians. The Morenos live on former mission lands, but Jackson does not condemn them for this. In fact, it is the decision of the Americans to to restore the mission holdings that breaks Father Salvierderra's heart. Jackson depicts the Moreno rancho with its chapel as carrying on some of the paternal and religious function of the missions. Rancho-era Indians labor as self-sufficient workers in a mutually beneficial economic relationship with the landowners. The rancheros protect the Indian settlements against the encroachment of Americans.

Still, one can detect Jackson's ambivalence toward Mexican California. Each member of the Moreno household is flawed in some way--the Senora is wrathful, Felipe effete, the servants scheming. Jackson refers to the rancho period as "half barbaric, half elegant, wholly generous and free-handed." The rancheros may have been picturesque, but they lacked the Franciscans' zeal and sense of purpose. The implication that this indolent lifestyle deserved to perish no doubt comforted Jackson's American audience.

The majority of *Ramona* concerns itself with the decimation of the California Indian following the 1850s incursion of American settlers. The saga of Ramona and Alessandro coincides in nearly every detail with McWilliams' account. He tells how Indian sources of food supply were disrupted, family life broken up, and settlements of long standing summarily evicted. The Indian villages moved toward the mountains and deserts; many Indians gathered in the towns and drank. There they were paid only half the going wage or were paid in wine. These injustices led to an Indian "undercurrent of resentment (that) precluded even the thought of assimilation." Jackson believes that the essentially moral nature of the American settler broke down under the pressures of frontier life. Had he not been blinded by greed, he would have realized that the padres had cultivated incipient Yankees from pliable, noble Indian raw material like Alessandro. *Ramona* thus reinforces late-nineteenth century American values even while castigating the American settler.

In the last analysis, Jackson's novel reveals more about American attitudes in the 1880s than it does about the missions, the ranchos, or the American conquest of California. The hero Alessandro symbolizes qualities associated with the traditional work ethic. Ramona is a naively pure-hearted, quintessentially Victorian heroine. American disdain for poor Mexicans, as cited by McWilliams, appears in Jackson's blatantly low regard for them. By 1880, ninety percent of the Indian population of California had disappeared. The novel romanticizes a people that has been safely vanquished. McWilliams attributes the popular success of *Ramona* to the crass motives of Southern California tour operators and real estate speculators. It can be less cynically interpreted as an attempt to make sense of and atone for the recent past. Helen Hunt Jackson's *Ramona* may not be good history, or good fiction, but it is an ambitious exercise in cultural expiation.

THE READER'S TURN:

1. How much do you learn from this paper about the historical background or context in which the events of Jackson's story take place?
2. What does the student writer mean when she says that the novel "romanticizes" the Indians?
3. According to the student writer, how do later historians "corroborate" Jackson's story; how do they present a conflicting or different picture?
4. What parts of Jackson's story do you think might appeal to a modern reader; what parts might seem too old-fashioned or "Victorian"?
5. How were you taught American history? Do you think the picture you were given of the country's past was too idealized or too grimly realistic?

WRITING TOPICS 11

Critical writing is designed to steer us toward literature worth reading and to help us gain a fuller understanding and appreciation of it. (Some critical writing is designed to steer us away from literature that is trashy, superficial, or insincere.) The best critical writing helps us become more receptive, more responsive readers. Topics like the following give you an opportunity to share your discoveries as a reader with other readers.

1. The Poetry of Love: Probably the best-known nineteenth-century love poem is Elizabeth Barrett Browning's "How do I love thee? Let me count the ways." Find the poem in a standard anthology. Then pair it with a poem about love written in the twentieth century. Compare the two.
2. The Central Character: Some of the best-known short stories focus on a central character. The story may revolve around a person who is strange and puzzling, or provocative and infuriating, or perfectly ordinary. In a collection of outstanding short stories find a story focused on a major character. You may want to choose a story by Nathaniel Hawthorne, Ernest Hemingway, Flannery O'Connor, Katherine Anne Porter, or Joyce Carol Oates. Help other readers understand the central character.
3. Family Drama: Many of the great plays in the history of drama have focused on relationships within the family. Such plays range from Sophocles' *Oedipus Rex* and Shakespeare's *Hamlet* through Ibsen's *Wild Duck* to Tennessee Williams' *Glass Menagerie* and Lorraine Hansberry's *Raisin in the Sun*. Write about the way one such play holds up the mirror to the family as the setting or as a major force in people's lives.

4. To Look at Nature: Writers have written about nature as a hostile force or as a healing influence. Write about a poem or story in which the author's view of nature plays a major role. Or compare and contrast two poems or stories in which our relation to the natural world is a major theme.

5. A Plea for Empathy: A basic function of imaginative literature is to widen our horizons, to make us share imaginatively in experiences different from our own. When readers first read James Baldwin's *Notes of a Native Son* or Ralph Ellison's *Invisible Man*, many of them felt that for the first time they were beginning to understand what it was like to be black in a white society. Write about a work (fiction, biography, autobiography) that has had a similar effect on you. Write about a work that helped you understand what it means to be black, Puerto Rican, native American, an immigrant, or a woman. Or a writer may have helped you understand what it means to be a Catholic, or gay, or a Vietnam vet.

Part Four

Essays for Peer Review

Most writers do not write in a vacuum. Often their writing assumes its final shape only after they have tried out tentative ideas or trial drafts on friends, colleagues, editors, or reviewers. In many writing classes today, students profit from feedback from their peers at different stages of the writing process. How receptive and how helpful a critic are you of other students' writing?

12
Evaluation: Editor for a Day

The student papers in the following set have been edited for possible inclusion in a collection of student writing. You be the judge: Which of these would you include, and which would you keep out—and why? Rank the five entries from strongest to weakest, and compare and discuss your rankings with those of your classmates. What kind of revision do you think is needed to improve the weaker essays?

Prepare editorial comments for each paper. Try to point out both strengths and weaknesses. Use the following review of minimum *revision strategies* as a possible guide. How well has each writer heeded advice like the following?

- Get to the issue early—dispense with long evasive or roundabout introduction; start with a striking *example or anecdote*.

- Take a stand—When all the pro and con is sorted out, what are you trying to tell your reader? Spell out your main point early in the paper. Remember the reader who asks: What is this all about? What is the point?

- Push toward specifics—translate issue and ideas into revealing incidents, into what people say and do. Pile on extra *real-life examples*.

- Mark off major stages—signal major turning points; spell out the logical connections between one major chunk of material and the next. Remove weak transitions using *also* or *another*—ask instead: *Why* is this in here?

- Consider reshuffling sections for a better flow—boil down your overall strategy to a 3-point or 4-point outline to see if you need a more logical sequence from then to now, or from cause to effect.

- End on a strong note—save a clincher example or striking quote for the last.

The Cruelty of Children's Athletics

Although organized sports has obvious physical benefits, the emotional effects of fierce competition can be quite negative. The children who learn not to take competition very seriously can be successful if they can also avoid the impenetrable cliques, the false hopes raised by coaches and parents, and the vicious rivalry among their peers. Being a quiet but very observant child I watched these poor values ruin the attitudes of many young women through my nine years as a competitive swimmer.

It is common for many sporting teams to begin the children very young. Swim clubs draft recruits as young as six years old for the "eight and under" group. Practices are held every night and A.A.U. (Amateur Athletic Union) meets held nearly every weekend. This constant contact leads to very strong cliques of children who feel that they are more talented than their classmates. These children often do not let new people into the group if they decide they do not like them. Although they may be good for the team, new joiners can be forced to quit because the members of these cliques are cruel to them. One young girl, Marcia, joined our club when she was eleven years old. Because she started later than most of us, she had to go through a sort of initiation process. One of the older members, Gail, pretended to be a friend. At her first meet, Marcia became confused when her event was announced. Instead of leading her to the correct place, Gail told Marcia that she was to wait outside of the school until the coach would call her. Marcia was skeptical but did as Gail instructed. She waited in the (Wisconsin) January cold wearing a damp sweatsuit for half an hour before the coach found her and brought her inside to where she belonged. By that time little icicles had formed on her hair; she was shivering uncontrollably. The others in the club found it very amusing. When questioned by the coach, Gail denied having anything to do with the situation and the coach believed her. The "jokes" continued, and, by the end of the season, Marcia had quit the club.

Gail, however, remained as one of the top athletes in the state. She was thirteen years old and, according to her parents and coaches, Olympic-bound. Her mother took her out of school nearly every Thursday and Friday throughout the season to travel to all corners of the country to compete with the best of her age group. By age sixteen, though, she had "peaked" and even some girls in the club could beat her. At first she became bitter and resentful, tearing up the copy of <u>Swimmer's World</u> magazine the time it did a story on the new Olympic hopefuls. She had gotten to know some of them at meets around the country, but her name was not among theirs. Although she was intelligent, she had fallen behind in school and did not go to college as her teachers suggested. "I just don't think I could do it," she told them. She refused even to try.

The lessons Gail did learn were the ones taught by the coaches and other swimmers. Coaches lie about the fastest times of the swimmers to get them into heats with faster swimmers. They feel that it would speed improvement. The swimmers lie to each other. It is not uncommon for swimmers of different clubs to chat before a race. One will ask, "What's your best time for this event?" The other, with countless achievement patches adorning her sweatsuit, replies, "Oh, I'm not very good, really." The she flexes and stretches her muscles to warm up, and for her rival to see. These little games are meant to confuse and worry the competition into doing poorly, which is called "psyching out" the rivals.

It is not the intent of coaches to raise false hopes for the athletes, or to teach them to lie. Unfortunately, too often that is exactly what results from their behavior.

Today's Homeless

The homeless are a group of people who are often stereotyped as bums, derelicts, and dropouts. These stereotypes do not fit the realities. To understand homelessness today, one must understand who these people are and why they are poor and why their poverty takes the distinctive form of having nowhere to live. There have been decisive changes that have taken place in the circumstances that promote and perpetuate homelessness in the United States.

We need to look back during the sixties when deinstitutionalization in our country emptied out our mental institutions and placed our mentally ill back into our communities. Deinstitutionalization was not a bad idea itself, but in execution, the reality bore little resemblance to the ideals. The depopulation of the mental hospitals--from 557,000 in 1956 to 133,550 by 1980 (U.S. Bureau of the Census, 1984)--was never complemented by the resources needed to make community placement a workable reality. Specifically, the network of appropriate housing and support services failed to materialize. Even for a great number of people who were housed, it was not uncommon to have such arrangements disrupted. Such a population unused to living on its own is an easy target for landlords seeking more "desirable" tenants. Sometimes these individuals were unable to manage budgeting their money and this contributed to their displacement. Many were unable to fill in the proper forms to receive food stamps or public assistance. In late 1983, the Social Security Administration terminated benefits to almost half a million of the disabled (New York Times Dec. 10, 83). Studies have shown that most often the loss of benefits was due to the inability of the recipient to challenge the ruling, and not to a legitimate weeding from the ranks of those who have recovered (Mental Health Law Project 1982). The mentally ill who roughly represent 11 percent of those receiving disability benefits were overrepresented among those who were terminated by a factor of three (New York Times Sep. 9, 82).

Another group of the homeless are our unemployed--both skilled and unskilled individuals. The changes in unemployment insurance legislation implemented in 1981 placed severe restrictions on the payment of extended benefits. According to a Brookings Institution study, fewer than half of newly jobless workers in 1982 received unemployment benefits. In September 1983, with over 9.8 million still officially unemployed, only 32.8 percent were collecting unemployment benefits of any kind. Once out of work, today's unemployed are more likely to stay jobless for extended periods of time.

Others among the homeless and hungry are part of the dependent non-working poor. Despite the increase in poverty, from 1980 through early 1984, programs such as welfare, energy assistance, and food stamps were reduced 16.4 percent, while other non-human services increased by 24.5 percent.

Lastly, there is a small segment of our society made up of people who have dropped out from our mainstream mode. These people choose not to operate in a competitive mode of life. They feel that it is morally wrong for them to participate in a society that promotes profits over people. They do not want public assistance. They want only to live on land and grow their own food and operate in a barter system of existence.

The problem of the growing number of homeless is not going away. Perhaps we need to allow for a more non-competitive way of existence for certain segments of our society. The billions of dollars allocated for our star wars game could house and feed all of our homeless and create meaningful creative work for our able unemployed individuals. All of the above groups have rights in regard to basic existence--food and housing. It has become increasingly apparent that the problem of homelessness has less to do with personal inadequacy than it does with resource scarcity. The homeless are not asking for summer homes on Lake Tahoe. They only want a small fragment of our American Dream and their dignity as fellow human beings.

The Essence of Practicality

This essay will analyze the practical person in comparison to the creative person. It will cover the occupational and educational aspects, and the brain of the creative and practical person. It will show how we often integrate practicality and creativity to achieve a final product.

A practical person has a strong educational background. An education is needed to learn the practical logistics of an occupation. Practicality is learned. It has boundaries and is confined to method. Repairs, formulas, and logic need to be learned to achieve a desired effect. A scientist obtains an effect by studying.

The mechanic of a Boeing 747 sees every little detail of the airplane's engine. He goes by the book when fixing airplanes. Indeed, it would be very hazardous to add a creative fixture to the airplane's engine; therefore, the mechanic's job is a practical occupation. In contrast, Henry Ford built his own concept of the car; Ford was creative in conceptualizing the automobile. Car builders, such as the lowriders, could be considered creative; nevertheless, when we are repairing a vehicle the mechanical operations have to be practical. There are other occupations where practicality would be a strong asset. One would want a practical surgeon for triple bypass heart surgery.

It may be said that the practical person uses the left hemisphere of the brain, which follows a logical, linear, and methodical pattern. The left hemisphere of the brain perceives small detail, for example, a broken gasket. The practical person works sequentially. Tearing down the motor to get to the broken gasket is a strict process. As a result, being practical is being aware of the outcome or results. My mother prosaically fills out her expense forms. If she kept an imaginative account of her expenses it would not be accurate.

On the other hand, the creative person is intricate. Some believe creativity should evolve from oneself, whereas education forces one to go into a definite direction. As a result, artists are not heavily educated in a confining institution. Though techniques are helpful to artists, they do not need a degree to paint. The creative person is known as being artistic. Many people believe creativity is self-expression. And, sometimes the creative thought process may be so intricate the outcome is unknown, although fully conceptualized by the artist. It is difficult to perceive an audience's reaction; therefore, the creative person often takes chances--chances doctors and mechanics do not take.

Studies show that the right hemisphere of the brain talks in images and pictures. It is unlike the practical, linear, methodical, and logical left hemisphere. The right hemisphere is without limits and has no boundaries. The creative person has to be able to brainstorm without confinement. The creative person relies on imagery and analogy to produce expression. Many times a creative person is thrown into the limelight because she has created something new.

The creative person uses the right hemisphere of the brain to design, for example, a stained glass window; however, the actual process of building the window is painstakingly methodical. Sometimes practicality and creativity go hand and hand. Learning to use the computer I had to memorize a process of steps to get to my program. It is practical because it is methodical. Although I use my practical abilities to start up this word processor, I use my creative abilities to write this essay, though I am being analytic. Many times it takes practice to reach creativity. When people learn to paint, it would be much to their advantage to learn the methods of mixing paint before the actual execution of a painting is achieved. Furthermore, a surgeon's operation in all practicality may be perceived as creative when a significant breakthrough in science has been made to help defeat heart disease. For example, the invention of the pacemaker--a device that artificially stimulates the heart if it drops below 60 beats per minute--is a creative concept, but building a pacemaker is a practical process. In short, it is true, that many times creativity can lead to practicality and vice versa.

An Introduction to Prejudice

Waiting in line for lunch, I turned around after being hit on the shoulder by my fellow second-grader. At eight years old, we'd play around tapping each other on the arm, and I'd be extra careful because I was always bigger and stronger than my classmates in elementary school. But he continued to hit my arm as if angry about something. I warned my Asian friend that if he kept hitting me I'd hit him hard. When he continued, I hit him in the stomach; he doubled over and began crying. A guilty feeling ran through me, and if I could've taken back that punch I would have, although he did deserve it. My teacher, Mrs. Muramoto, saw him crying and asked what happened--he told her that I hit him, nothing else--then pinned me against the wall outside of a classroom. She was a short Japanese woman and probably weighed close to 200 pounds. She spoke a version of English that most Hawaiian natives spoke when she said, "How you like me to hit you in 'da stomach, how you like 'dat, big haole boy?" <u>Haole</u> is the Hawaiian native's equivalent of the mainland's <u>honkey</u>. I tried to explain what actually happened, but she didn't listen at all. For punishment I sat in the principal's office all day. I was one of the few white pupils who attended Noelani Elementary School, so I quickly learned what it's like to be a minority. Once I told a classmate that he needed a bath. Later his older brother, a sixth grader, approached me after school, shoved me a few times and told me to watch what I said to his brother, then called me a "haole flatface." At the time I didn't know exactly what that meant but I knew it was an insult.

In Hawaii I was treated differently than most kids. I had few close friends because I was white, so when I came back to the mainland I made it a point to make friends with those who were alienated--I didn't want anyone to feel the same way I did. I was very sensitive toward minorities, until I moved to my present neighborhood. Cars are being broken into and ripped off. Once my roommate, Steve, saw a man trying to break into a car. Steve yelled, "Hey! What are you doing?" The guy reached into his coat as if he was reaching for a gun and said, "Hey, what?" To that Steve said, "Hey, nothing" and left. In another incident two people entered the back of a fraternity house and tried to steal a keg of beer. The members caught them, took the keg back, and let them go, which may have been a mistake. Within an hour their microwave oven was stolen.

Every such crime in my neighborhood that I have heard about seems to involve minorities. I hate to pinpoint any group of people, but the more crimes I see and hear about the more prejudice I feel, especially after witnessing what happened the other night just outside my bedroom window.

I heard voices yelling and I looked out my window to see a white student lying on his back, his shirt having been ripped off his body. Three black boys and a black girl were kicking him and yelling at him to give them his money. In a panic of not knowing what to do, I ran two flights upstairs to find my roommates. Then I poked my head out of the third-story window and told them to leave the victim alone and get off our property or they'd be arrested. One of them, the apparent leader and probable instigator, looked up at me, the victim's wallet in hand, and swore at me as if he'd been interrupted while doing something perfectly legitimate.

After being pushed around and alienated as a Caucasian in Hawaii, I had become sensitive to the feelings of the outsider. But I am seeing my feelings of sympathy toward minorities change slowly into feelings of hostility and prejudice.

Sometimes a Hidden Cancer

I'm just a few weeks back from a visit to Idaho, the state where I was born, grew up, and where my family lives still. Is prejudice on the decline? During my visit, I read endless articles in the News Tribune, the local paper, about the Aryan World Congress. Since 1979, these white supremacists have met in Hayden Lake, Idaho, every summer except one to discuss the establishment of a racist "territorial sanctuary," a white homeland, in Idaho, Washington, Oregon, Montana, and Wyoming. The Congress is hosted by the Church of Jesus Christ Christian (Aryan Nations), one of the growing numbers of inter-related groups who adhere to a doctrine known as Christian Identity. The Identity movement holds that the Aryans of Europe and North America are the true children of Israel. They see the Jews as imposters, the children of the Devil, who have caused all the world's problems from the banking system to communism to every major war since 1861 to inner-city crime. Identity followers believe that the Devil's plan is to mongrelize the Aryans out of existence.

This summer, the big news about the Congress was the fire control ordinance that prevented the annual cross burning. It was a dry year; the county wasn't giving fire permits, so the Aryans had a cross lighting. The "fiery" cross, summoning all Christian clansmen to war, was lit up with electric light bulbs. One participant was quoted in the News Tribune as saying, "Compared to last year, it was like going from a forest fire to a barbecue."

In the meantime, in a small town, my sister-in-law, a white woman married to a black man, bought a dog so she could let her little daughter and son play outside. She watches out the windows. (Her mother told her when she wanted to get married that the children would be the ones to suffer. Her father didn't talk to her for two years. He punished her for marrying a descendant of Noah's son Ham, one cursed by Noah to be forever a servant.) Her husband delivers corn chips to stores in redneck-run towns where men walk the streets wearing arm patches showing a shield, a sword, and a twisted cross. Is prejudice on the decline?

In a newspaper interview on July 19 (the Congress was held July 11-12) in the Coeur d'Alene Press, Rev. Richard G. Butler, head of the Church of Jesus Christ Christian, said he didn't oppose the existence of racial minorities but feared for the future of the white gene pool. He said, "I don't hate rattlesnakes. I just don't want my bed full of rattlesnakes. They have their place and I have mine."

All this happens while we watch "The Cosby Show" on Thursday night, acclaim <u>The Color Purple</u>, officially celebrate Martin Luther King, Jr. Day, and listen to Oprah Winfrey as she discusses current events in her strong, aggressive way.

Some people might say those crazies in Idaho are just a few extremists who don't have the numbers or strength to carry out their plan. Their numbers are relatively small. According to a spokesman only 250 participants pre-registered to attend this year's Congress; however, a quick view over the nation's newspapers and magazines for the last five years reveals that the people who are in the Ku Klux Klan, the Nazi Party, and Aryan Nations, Posse Comitatus, the Covenant, Sword and Arm of the Lord, the White Patriot Party, SS Action Group, the White Student Union, and numerous other white supremacist organizations are radical hard-liners who have an inclination toward violence. Their members have been charged with bombings, counterfeiting, robberies, murders, and plotting revolution.

Is prejudice on the decline? No, it is not. Its shape is different. We don't see anything as blatant as slavery, and since the Civil Rights Movement, segregation is no longer legally tolerated, but crude prejudices do exist and discrimination does occur.

Along with the articles on the Aryan Nations Congress, I read about the human rights festival that has been held in Coeur d'Alene for the last two years as an antidote to the Aryan Congress. This year at the celebration organized to promote human understanding and harmony, the leaders wouldn't let a Wiccan religious leader and self-proclaimed witch sing folk songs. A group of witches angered by this decision staged a demonstration at the festival. The organizer of the demonstration was quoted in the <u>News Tribune</u> as saying, "If they are going to have a human rights celebration, they ought to practice what they preach."